THE
COMPLETE
MODEL

FOR POSITIVE
BEHAVIOR MANAGEMENT

A TRANSFORMATIONAL GUIDE
FOR PARENTS AND EDUCATORS

DINA AL-HIDIQ ZEBIB

Book Layout by: Intentional Media
Cover Design by: Prodesign360

ISBN: 978-2955861301

ABOUT THE AUTHOR

Dina Al-Hidiq Zebib is an award-winning Certified PBIS (Positive Behavior Interventions and Supports) Coach, Life Coach, Transformation Coach and Solution-Focused Coach. She is an active professional development trainer and supports many educators and schools. She holds a Bachelor's degree in Education, a Master's degree in Clinical Psychology, a Certificate in Coaching for Multi-Tier System of Supports for Behavior, and certificates in Life Coaching, Transformation Coaching and Solution-Focused Coaching. She has worked as a teacher in schools with children of various ages and with students who have special needs. She also taught adolescents and adults in universities and educational centers, and worked as a school counselor and a director of a child education center. She currently provides Positive Behavior Support coaching and consultancy services, and presents professional development workshops internationally for educators and parents. She is married and has two children. In addition to coaching, consultancy and training, she is the author of the award-winning novel *CROSSROADS*.

To my mother Ghada and my father Bassam,
You raised me with love and positivity.
I am what I am because of you.

To my husband Hussein, my eternal love and partner.
You are my support and encouragement.

To my boys, Faris and Amir, my most precious treasures.
You are my heart and inspiration.

CONTENTS

INTRODUCTION 1

Chapter One... 7
CONTEMPLATE AND REFLECT

Chapter Two 15
OPENHEARTEDLY LISTEN

Chapter Three 21
MAKE STRONG CONNECTIONS

Chapter Four...35
PLAN YOUR PRIORITIES

Chapter Five.. 51
LEAD THE LEARNING THROUGH DIRECT TEACHING

Chapter Six... 67
EMPOWER THROUGH ACKNOWLEDGEMENT

Chapter Seven...83
TACTFULLY CORRECT

Chapter Eight..99
EVOLVE AND TRANSFORM

INTRODUCTION

Humans thrive in positive environments.
Then why do we keep creating climates that are negative?

I have always been fascinated with child development and deeply concerned about the psychological, social and emotional well-being of children. The first educational conference that I attended in the late-nineteen nineties was on Global Education for a Child-Friendly School. The topics that captivated me were about being positive, proactive and preventive when managing behavior. I still remember how the sentence "Catch them being good!" rang in my ears and helped focus my efforts on being a positive and proactive educator. I was still young and a fresh graduate from the school of education at the American University of Beirut. I had already grown into an advocate and speaker for children's well-being in their homes, classrooms and schools. But that moment at the conference was an inspirational one. My mind and heart had opened up to the truth of how we should raise our children and students—positively and proactively. We should be positive and not negative. We must be proactive and not reactive. That one statement captured the gist of what our efforts as educators and parents should be oriented towards—Catching Them Being Good.

Today, after having been a school teacher, university instructor, counselor, coach and trainer, advocating for children's best interests, and supporting others by delivering the best research-

1

based educational practices, I feel the urge to write a book about how we, as educators and parents, should be with our children and students.

As humans, what is our ultimate goal in life? To be happy and content; to avoid pain and gain pleasure; to connect socially; to experience meaning and relevance in our life; to raise a happy family; to enjoy a life of peace, stability and safety; to be successful; to gain recognition; to be respected members of our community.

As educators, what is our ultimate goal in life? All of the above—as well as ensuring that our students are successful, academically and behaviorally.

How can we achieve these goals? What do we need to do to actualize our purposes in life? How can we learn about what truly matters to us? What do we need to do to learn more about ourselves, priorities, purposes and beliefs? We need to first gain insight into our inner selves and learn what truly matters to us. We need to gain awareness about the powerful impact we have on ourselves and others. We need to self-assess our beliefs and behaviors. We must self-reflect in order to learn and begin transforming into better individuals. We have to understand the power of positivity in shaping our lives and the lives of others. We need to tap into our internal spring of positive emotions that we all possess, but are not always aware of. We need to implement systems with fidelity if we expect to have any order in the world.

My book will not delve into any spiritual, psychic or energy healing approaches. It will simply present you with probing questions for you to reflect on your own practices, and discuss the steps that you can implement, systematically, at home, in your classroom and in school, to ensure that your students and children are addressed and catered to in a positive, proactive and preventive way. Why? In order to raise children who are happy, successful, emotionally intelligent, and conscientious citizens of the world. Our world badly needs better, kinder, and more virtuous people. It is us—the adults in their lives—that can influence them now for a better present and a more promising future.

In my work as a coach, I have had the wonderful opportunity to work with and support community and international schools, as well as individuals from various international backgrounds. Every interaction is intriguing for me, and an incredible chance for me to look at child development from a global perspective.

A question I frequently ask myself is: Why do we have so much negativity in the world? Why do some people choose to do evil things rather than good deeds? Why do some students fight and bully each other? Why do some children lie, cheat and revel in wrongdoing? Why do some adults want to stay the same, but expect children to change? Why do some adults believe that making children feel bad will lead them to being good? Why do some adults feel they have the right to use their power over children to make them feel bad? Why do some adults abuse the innocence of children who would actually believe anything grown-ups might show them or say to them?

In my modest opinion, it is due to a lack of positive, proactive and preventive set of practices while growing up. Who is responsible for providing these practices? It should be us—the adults in those children's lives—their parents, educators, coaches, administrators, etc. Honestly, are you putting enough effort towards supporting your children's behavior? Are you catching children being good? Or are you reveling in your victory for catching them being bad? Are these feelings of your own victory allowing you to flourish? Do they truly make you feel like a better person? How would you feel if you were humbler about winning the battle now, but celebrated your triumph through the successes of your children?

3

Wouldn't it be an actual success if you were to celebrate everybody's successes, instead of just yours?

The lessons presented in this book are those derived from my educational practices within a positive, proactive and preventive behavior management approach that I have implemented for many years with students in schools in various countries, as well as with my own children. They are also practices that fit in with any positive and proactive behavior approach that you may be implementing in your schools or homes. These lessons present themselves as effective habits for your personal transformation as adults, as well as for use with children at home, and with students at school for the management of their behavior.

In this book, I will present the COMPLETE Model that I have created as a transformational approach for parents and educators. COMPLETE is an acronym that summarizes the steps that should be followed for successful implementation of positive behavior management. Every chapter will introduce and explain a step from the model, as well as provide examples and tools to guide implementation. In chapter eight, you will find the entire model with a summary of implementation, to help guide your efforts for the complete process of the COMPLETE Model.

Below is a summary of my COMPLETE transformational model for behavior management:

C	**Contemplate and Reflect**
O	**Openheartedly Listen**
M	**Make Strong Connections**
P	**Plan Your Priorities**
L	**Lead the Learning through DIRECT Teaching**
E	**Empower Through Acknowledgement**
T	**Tactfully Correct**
E	**Evolve and Transform**

I truly believe in magic. With heartfelt positivity and wholehearted commitment to providing the best practices and opportunities for our children, magic can truly happen. If you want to see changes in your children, begin by changing yourself. Tap into your internal source of positive emotions and genuine concern for your children and students. Truly believe that it is you and your behavior that can impact their development, their psychological, social and emotional well-being, as well as their academic and behavioral successes.

Let's be accountable for our behaviors. Let's make a stronger effort to positively support our children. Let's anticipate, hand-in-hand, that we can create a better future. This future will be determined by the positive efforts we make now to raise better children that we will send out into the world tomorrow.

The following chapters will discuss the systems that you must set in place as you cater to the needs of children. In my chapters, I will use the word 'children' to imply 'your own children as well as your students'. The age group I will be referring to includes school-age children, from the ages of four until seventeen.

Every chapter will begin with probing questions for you to reflect upon before you begin reading the chapter. As I explain the procedures and strategies, I will also present tools that will help you better understand and implement the strategies, in order to become better providers of positive, proactive and preventive practices.

My purpose in this book is to present to you my COMPLETE Model in a concise and step-by-step practical educational guide, which I am hoping will be inspiring and enlightening enough to allow transformation, and practical enough to allow efficient implementation. I hope you find the joy, inspiration and drive to transform as you move yourself forward, while providing the best care for your children.

Let's dream of a better world...let's work to make it happen...let's follow the COMPLETE Model to change the world and make it a better place.

Chapter One
CONTEMPLATE AND REFLECT

*Self-reflection is perhaps one of the most
powerful change agents we can ever employ.*

**What kind of environment do you think children need,
in order to grow up into
positive, caring and responsible world citizens?
What is your attitude towards behavior management?
What is your attitude towards using a positive approach
to support child behavior?
How willing are you to encourage children to behave well?
How strongly do you believe that your behavior
as adults can impact children's behavior?
How willing are you to change your behavior
to bring about change in child behavior?**

As parents, we are the main teachers for our children. We help them learn how to walk by doing a lot of things. We provide them with an infant walker toy, we help them use their hands and arm muscles to pull themselves up from a solid counter top, and we hold their hands as they take their first steps. We also teach them how to begin eating independently by giving them dry snacks to hold and munch on, as well as giving them a baby spoon and a bowl of food so they could begin learning how to scoop food and find their way to their mouths. We also teach them how to speak their first words by articulating, repeating and speaking to them. We teach them how to ride a bicycle, how to say hello to others and how to make new friends. We teach them how to be wary of strangers and how to say 'please' and 'thank you'. We teach them values and instill in them life principles. The process of teaching our children and the repertoire of skills and values we provide are endless, beginning right from the day they are born.

As teachers and workers in the field of education, we teach our students how to read letters then words; we teach them how to trace, write letters, words, sentences and stories; we teach them how to count, add, subtract, multiply and divide; we teach them fundamental math skills and various concepts; we teach them how to problem-solve; we teach them physical activities and sports; we teach them how to read music, play instruments and appreciate music; we instill in them the love of art and teach them art and design concepts; we provide the necessary interventions whenever they fall behind or need individualized support; we scaffold instruction and differentiate the learning process to help them all succeed in learning.

However, with all that we consciously and purposefully do and explicitly teach our children and students, do we dedicate the same time and effort to teaching behavior? Do we include the teaching of behavioral expectations, classroom and school procedures into our lesson plans of math, reading, writing, PE, music, art, etc.? Do we explicitly teach children what their behavior is expected to be like? Do we proactively anticipate what misbehaviors might be and preventively teach them how to behave? Do we 'catch them being good' instead of 'catching them doing wrong'? When they fall behind in their behavior and do not behave according to behavioral expectations, do we go back, intervene and reteach? Do we acknowledge and celebrate good behavior often, or do we only remember to punish, reprimand and scold?

Sadly, it is quite common that when children's behavior falls behind, we tend to punish, reprimand and scold. We are reactive instead of being proactive; we fail to lay the foundation for prevention, and choose to use punitive methods when they fail; we forget the power of positive interactions, and feel more at ease with negative interactions. We believe that we must make children feel bad for them to become good.

What are the reasons for this? It could be many things. Firstly, many of us grew up in a disciplinary environment, which was reactive and used punishment as a means to teach children good behavior. Secondly, it could be that people do not know how to implement positive, proactive and preventive systems that create stable and predictable environments in classrooms, schools and homes. Either way, we must begin challenging our mindsets to believing that children must be explicitly taught how to behave, acknowledged and rewarded when they do the right thing, taught about consequences of personal choices, respected as capable individuals, allowed to flourish in a positive environment that believes, expects and anticipates that they will be successful, and encouraged to be their best.

What do you remember from your childhood? Close your eyes and transport back to the distant past when you were a young child. What memories do you have? When you think about the moments that were full of joy, pride and success, what emotions do you experience? How good does that make you feel right now, remembering the positive experiences and sensing the joyful sentiments? Try to remember the negative incidents when you did something wrong. Were you treated badly? Were you scolded or punished? Did you become a better person from the painful discipline inflicted on you? How about if you were treated with dignity when you did something wrong. Were you taught about what other choices you could have made? Were you encouraged to try again? Did the adults in your life support you and tell you that they believed you could do the right thing? Were you gently allowed to self-assess and self-reflect on your wrong choices, and encouraged to make better decisions next time? Were you treated with a positive attitude when you made better choices later? Did that make you feel empowered?

Reflect upon your own past experiences and examine your current beliefs. Do you truly believe that children will thrive in a positive environment? Or, do you believe that children must be punished? Do you believe in smiling or frowning? Do you believe you do not have to acknowledge good behavior in children because that is how they should be behaving? Or, do you believe that acknowledging good behavior will reinforce the desired behavior to occur again? Do you imagine that you must practice on your children what was practiced on you?

If you believe, have begun to believe, or are willing to believe that children thrive in positive environments, that we, as adults, have a responsibility to teach children behavioral expectations as well as how to behave, that we need to consider changing *our* behaviors if we are to anticipate any positive changes in child behavior, then please read on. Begin by conducting the Self-Interview in Tool 1.1.

Tool 1.1

SELF-INTERVIEW

Spend quiet time alone and conduct an interview with yourself using the following questions:

1. Try to recall memories from your childhood.

At School:

a. How were you treated when you did something wrong? How did you feel?
b. Did your behavior improve as a result?
c. Was there a time when you were not punished when you did something wrong? How did you feel?
d. Were you empowered to behave in a better way next time?
e. Who is the teacher you remember the most?
f. Why? What do you remember about that teacher?

At Home:

g. How were you treated when you did something wrong? How did you feel?
h. Did your behavior improve as a result?
i. Was there a time when you were not punished when you did something wrong? How did you feel?
j. Were you empowered to behave in a better way next time?
k. Who is the adult you remember the most?
l. Why? What do you remember about that adult?

2. Think about your life right now:

At School (if you are an educator):

a. What is the general climate like? Is it a happy, confident and overall positive climate?

b. Is there a great deal of misbehavior?
    i. Why do you think so? What could be the reasons?
    ii. If there is a lot of misbehavior, what could you do to change this?

c. Describe to yourself what you look like around your students.
    i. Do you smile or frown more often?
    ii. Do you tend to respond to them more when they behave well or misbehave?
    iii. Do you consider yourself strict?
    iv. Do you take the time to engage with them in play, games or fun activities?
    v. What acts of kindness have you shown them this week?
    vi. How many times were you impatient with them this week?

At Home:

d. What is the general climate like? Is it a happy, confident and overall positive climate?

e. Is there a great deal of misbehavior?
    i. Why do you think so? What could be the reasons?
    ii. If there is a lot of misbehavior, what could you do to change this?

f. Describe to yourself what you look like around your children.
    i. Do you smile or frown more often?
    ii. Do you tend to respond to them more when they behave well or misbehave?
    iii. Do you consider yourself strict?
    iv. Do you take the time to engage with them in play, games or fun activities?
    v. What acts of kindness have you shown them this week?
    vi. How many times were you impatient with them this week?

3. In your opinion, do you think the world could benefit more from positive behaviors, such as joy, compassion, loyalty, honesty, love, friendship, peace, etc.?

4. Do you feel you could contribute in any way to making the world a better place?
5. How could you do that?
6. Where and with whom could you begin?

---

7. Do you think children benefit more from punishment or from forgiveness and encouragement? Why do you think so?

Chapter Two
OPENHEARTEDLY LISTEN

Happiness is a choice determined by
your positive thoughts and behaviors

What rituals do you practice to help you
listen to your inner voice?

How do you assess your behaviors, attitudes and beliefs?

How often do you conduct self-assessments
and self-reflections?

What feelings do you constantly experience?

Do you experience any negative emotions?

What events or experiences make you
feel these negative emotions?

What feelings would you like to experience more of?

What positive emotions have you recently felt?

What makes you feel positive?

Can you name some forms of positive emotions?

Getting in-tune with your inner self requires time, practice and conscious self-discipline. Listening to our inner voice is a skill that we need to develop if we aim to become more receptive to our needs and our children's. When we are in a constant rush to finish tasks and move on, we miss out on the most important duty we are responsible for, which is to cater to the needs of ourselves and others, as parents and educators. If we are in constant motion, without much thought about the purpose of our activities, we will not be conscious of our direction and will fail to achieve our goals. In our daily life, most of us lack the time needed to spend on introspection, self-assessment and self-reflection. Without assessment and reflection, we will not be able to develop ourselves as persons and professionals, nor will we be able to listen to our needs and the needs of our children and students.

In a world where we are overwhelmed with things to do, chores, long working hours, growing responsibilities and endless distractions, it is a great challenge to detach ourselves from the daily rush to be able to savor the moment and relish the here and now. It truly is a challenge.

So, how can we find the time to detach ourselves from the daily hustle of life, work, and responsibilities? If we aim to be the best caretakers and educators for our children and students, then we need to devote some time when we can detach ourselves from the world and look within ourselves.

When do you have a stretch of time when you can be alone? Do you have an opportunity for a break during the day when there are no distractions, impending responsibilities, or urgent obligations? It could be in the morning while drinking your coffee, or in the evening when you are unwinding right before going to bed. In my situation, this alone time is usually when I am unwinding during the evening, right before I go to bed. I have ritualized this time for myself, to look within myself, assess and reflect on my actions, attitudes and feelings. How did I feel today? How have I been feeling this past week and month? Am I satisfied with my performance? Am I catering to the needs of the others that I serve? Am I considerate to my needs and well-being? Was I negative in my feelings and behaviors with myself and others? Why? Have I experienced positive emotions today, this past week or month? What were they? Why did I experience them? What can I do more of to continue experiencing these positive emotions? What can I do less of to avoid the pain inflicted by the negative emotions? What are my priorities in life? Is my life moving along in synchrony with my goals, purposes and aspirations?

Practice this every day, or at least three times per week, during the time that you can devote for yourself. After some time, you will start gaining awareness into your own powers and how you are impacting yourself and others—the children you are responsible for.

As you become more aware of your inner voice and of your influence in the world, begin focusing on how you can grow your supply of positive emotions by cultivating your inner spring of heartfelt positivity. Everybody possesses this ingredient, but the supply can only grow when you tap into it and make a conscious effort to grow it. This is done by dedicating more focused effort to finding what makes you feel more positive and making a purposeful effort to experiencing those positive feelings.

On the next page, there is a tool that I created for you to use with a family member, partner or friend. It is a helpful tool for reflecting on the positive moments in your life, in order to allow yourself to be gradually dominated by positivity, nudging aside the negative feelings that put you down and demotivate you. The more positive you are, the more prepared you are to care for the well-being of yourself and your children and students. The discussion that you would have will uplift your mood and help you begin the shift towards a healthier, happier, and more positive person.

TOOL 2.1

Wellspring of Positive Emotions

Choose a quiet time and sit in a comfortable spot by yourself or with a family member, partner or friend. It could be in the sitting room of a home, or outdoors in a setting where you can sit and view beautiful scenery around you. Ask yourself these questions, or take turns to ask each other, alternating for each one. This way you could both share your thoughts about the same question at the same time. Choose as many questions as you like from the list.

1. Joy: What brings about feelings of happiness for you?

2. Gratitude: What do you feel grateful for?

3. Peace: Think about the last time you felt calm and peaceful.

4. Hope: What things in life make you hopeful?

5. Pride: What makes you proud?

6. Fun: When was the last time you laughed and had an enjoyable time?

7. Inspiration: What makes you feel inspired?

8. Love: When does your heart feel governed with love?

9. Compassion: What incident touched your heart and made you feel empathy?

10. Cooperation: When was the last time you lent a helping hand, without being asked?

11. Accomplishment: What accomplishments have you made? Name one.

12. Beauty: When was the last time you saw something beautiful? What was it and where?

13. Freedom: What does it mean to be free, in your personal opinion?

Chapter Three
MAKE STRONG CONNECTIONS

Our need to connect with others is as important as food and water.
Stop making contacts with others; start making connections.

What kind of social interactions do you seek?

How valuable and supportive are your social connections?

What do you feel when you are treated with respect and trust?

How empowered do you feel when you
receive support from others?

What are the benefits of building strong
relationships with others?

When was the last time you played a game with someone?

How attentive are you to others in your family,
classroom, school or social circle?

Connecting with your children at home, in your classroom or in school, is one of the most powerful approaches you could ever practice as a parent or educator. So what do we mean by connecting?

Neuroscience has revealed to us the importance for humans to connect socially with others. Research has shown that our need to connect is as important as food and water. Our brains are wired in such a way that our well-being depends on our social connections.

We all agree that we are social creatures. We live in groups called families and communities. We depend on a certain structure for satisfying our needs for food, shelter, safety, and social recognition. We feel pain when we are shunned by society and pleasure when we are admired by others. We all know how powerful peer influence is on children, and how children thrive on social bonds with adults. If these relationships were dysfunctional or broken in any way, children would suffer long-term health, psychological and emotional disorders as well as educational problems.

This means that we need to create high-quality connections for ourselves and for our children. How can we create these connections?

First of all, treat others with respect. Treat your children with respect. Even if they are children, it does not mean they do not feel or comprehend the positive emotions that come with feeling respected. When you belittle children, they will develop negative feelings towards you and end up resenting you. I constantly tell teachers that if a child does not like them, they will never be able to make the child listen to them. Children will develop a defense mechanism and 'block' the adults out. Even worse, those children might become defiant and disruptive, giving adults a very hard time.

Some teachers I have observed reprimand, yell at and scold children for the slightest mishap. The child misbehaved initially, and that was why they received the scolding. But, what did that child learn? That the teachers do not respect them; that they are terrible children who misbehaved and deserve to be disrespected. They are no longer motivated to fix their behavior and behave well next time, because their self-worth has been damaged. They feel that they are integrally bad, and that no matter what they do, they will be bad. So, they lose the motivation to try. This is a learned attitude, developed by adult behavior.

Remember when you reflected upon a question I asked you previously, about how you were treated as a child when you did something wrong. Did the positive support you received from the adults in your life when they believed you could do the right thing make you feel motivated to behave in a better way? Did the positive behavior support make you feel empowered?

As adults, we are not expected to be perfect, but we are expected to be more insightful and better at self-regulation than children, who are still in the process of growth, development and maturation. When we lose our temper with children and end up disrespecting them, we are only raising our personal flag of failure. We, as adults, who are supposed to know better—not be perfect— but be more equipped with functional decision-making tools, failed with ourselves and with our children. We are not expected to be perfect, but we are expected to do our best—the best that we possibly can, and continue to grow, develop and improve.

I did my children and students wrong on many instances in the past, and I know I can never be perfect. But, I kept on trying my best to improve and develop into a better and more responsible person. I apologized to others when I did them wrong. I cried to my children when I was impatient with them and did them wrong—and I admitted my faults to them. I told them how much I loved and cared about them and that was why I was willing to learn and do better next time. I was honest and real. I had their support and they had mine. We were all committed to respecting each other, being truthful and human.

When dealing with behavior problems, the best approach is to handle them in an objective and unemotional way. If you feel you are approaching a high-energy negative emotion, remove yourself immediately, or send the child you are in conflict with to another adult. If you are at home, ask your partner or an adult family member to sit with the child and have them conduct a 'Calming and Thinking Exercise' (see the tool section at the end of this chapter). As for you, if you can continue doing what you are doing calmly, do so. Or, you may want to go for a walk or a jog for ten minutes, to vent your high-energy negative emotions, and stabilize your mood again.

However, incidents of this sort do not necessarily indicate that the relationship has been severed. You can still correct the emotional experience by conferring with the child and being honest about what happened—but only after you have allowed enough time for both of you to calm down. Openness and honesty moves a relationship to whole new level, and this is where the social connections can grow deeper and stronger.

I cannot stress enough the importance of building strong relationships with children. As I mentioned before, respect, honesty and openness are essential for building those relationships. Refer to Tools 3.3 and 3.4 for strategies for building strong relationships.

Another crucial method is support. We need to communicate to our children that we are there to support them, to provide all that it takes for them to be successful. We often hear children say, "The teacher does not care about me," or "My mother does not care about anyone but herself." These are signals indicating that the children do not know that they have our support and commitment. If we do not explicitly tell them, and if we do not go out of our way to show them and prove to them, they will continue to doubt. Remind children continuously by telling them, "I care about you. I care about your success and well-being. My role is to support you and to provide you with whatever you need to be successful." Keep saying it to them; they will eventually believe it.

A few years ago, I was teaching English at the secondary school level. One of my classes was a grade twelve class. They were quite a handful and it was not an easy feat to coax them into coming to class or to do their work. So, I focused all my energy on connecting with them. I was attentive; I showed interest in their thoughts and listened to their concerns; I allowed them breathing space and did not try to control them; I showed them respect and treated them with kindness; I asked them how they wanted my support and I expressed to them how I expected them to be; I told them about the beautiful and promising adventures that awaited them the following year when they were off to college. They loved to eat, so I brought them snacks to munch on as they worked. I was different from other teachers, but that was why they admired me, followed expectations and were successful. I established a classroom climate where they wanted to be because they were heard, respected and cared for. They showed up to my class—and they did the work. They missed other classes, but they came to mine.

During the following year, I received a text message from one of those students who had moved to London to pursue his university education. He wrote, "Thank you, Mrs. Zebib, for all that you did for us. Thank you for all that you taught us and for caring about us. Whenever I have to write an essay, I remember you. You taught us well. You believed in us."

This is the acknowledgement that all of us educators like to hear.

One time, I had to cover for an absent teacher. It was a humanities class. The students were the twelfth graders that I taught, as well as one other student. That student that I did not teach gave me a hard time. He was defiant and disruptive. He refused to do any work and was disrespectful. I told him one thing, "It is your choice to be part of the class or not. The rest of the students want to do the work." I continued my lesson, and did not challenge him into a power struggle. He sat on the side and refused to participate.

At the end of the lesson, my students apologized for the behavior of the other student. "He doesn't know you. He doesn't know that you are such a kind and wonderful teacher. He is just being foolish. We apologize for his behavior." I had their respect and admiration.

At the end of that year, I was part of the graduation committee that was responsible for preparing the students for their big day. It was hard work, but a lot of fun. The students were ecstatic. I worked with every student to make sure they were ready for their momentous event—even the one who had been disrespectful. I guided and supported him, just as I did with everybody else.

On the day of their graduation, right before they walked up the stage, that student who had been disrespectful came up to me. He said he was sorry for that incident and that he shouldn't have behaved that way. He also thanked me for my support. He smiled and I could see the appreciation in his eyes. It was an incredible moment.

You can see how powerful it is to create strong connections with our children and students. What also strengthens these connections is to improve your support levels by asking them honestly: *What kind of support do you need from me? What could I do to make you feel that I am there for you? What would you like me to do to prove to you that I care about you and that I want you to be happy and successful?* Don't be afraid to ask such questions. Some adults refuse to ask such questions because they feel it diminishes their degree of authority over the children. But, what good is an authoritative figure if they cannot reach out and impact the behaviors of others? Fear will not change child behavior permanently, but respect, support and strong relationships will.

Listen to what they tell you and act on it. Whenever they are facing a problem and need your support, be there for them. This way, they will truly believe that they have your support, and they will develop trust, which is another crucial element for building strong relationships.

What about your presence? Are you truly there for your children when they communicate with you? Children have quite acute perceptions, and they can easily be aware of how present you are. When you are with your children at home or with your students at school, are you attentive to what they say and do? Do you affirm the interactions by communicating back to them to let them understand that you are listening? Are you actively and deeply listening to what they are saying? If you are not, they will realize that you do not care about developing the relationship between you. They will move on and you would have lost them. Attentive and active listening is powerful in strengthening the relationships you build with others. At the end of this chapter, there are listening and communication tips that you can practice to improve your presence with your children and students.

So you learned about several elements so far that strengthen your connections and relationships with children. There is one more thing I would like to add: Play. Life is serious and busy enough as it is, so why not include the element of play? I surveyed a group of middle-schoolers once and asked them about what they thought would strengthen their relationships with their teachers. Ninety percent said, "We would like opportunities to play with our teachers."

What about your own children? How many times do your children ask you to go up to their room to play with them? How many times do your children beg you to go outside to the garden to engage in an activity together? How uplifted do they feel when you take them out to the park and play a game of football together? How excited do they feel when you take them to the beach, swim, build a sand castle or go kayaking together? When was the last time you actually played with them?

Plan family activities for every week. Spend an afternoon or two playing a game together. Schedule a day out at the park or beach for the weekend. Go out and plant a few vegetables together in your garden or in the plant pot on your window sill. Watch funny videos together and laugh. Play charades or hangman. Get your rackets out and play a game of badminton. Join them in their favorite PlayStation game. Go ahead and do it—nurture a happy and strongly bonded family.

What about in your classroom? When was the last time you stopped teaching and decided to play a game with them? Games could also be used to reinforce learning, without having to tell the children that they are actually learning! When was the last time you went on a field trip with your students and played a game of tag? Have you ever actually played a game with them, outside of the classroom? When was the last time you laughed with your students? Have you ever actually laughed with them, or are you always very serious?

I still vividly remember the times when my teachers played and laughed with us. They were powerful moments and I felt more connected to them. Seeing them laugh and play with us made me feel closer to them and made me admire and love them more.

Go ahead and plan fun games as a closing task to your lesson. Plan a game with your students during break time. Celebrate their hard-work and good behavior by planning a field trip to the park. Sing songs or tell jokes on the bus. Organize a crazy hair day at school. Plan for fun, playful events and feel the connections grow.

TOOL 3.1

Calming and Thinking Exercise

The best approach when dealing with behavior problems is to handle them in an objective and unemotional way. So, when you see a child's misbehavior escalating, and you feel you are about to lose your patience, remove yourself immediately, or send the child you are in conflict with to be with another adult. If you are at home, ask your partner or adult family member to sit with the child and have them conduct this exercise. For younger children, have someone read them to the child who would respond verbally, draw a picture or write down their responses.

This tool is also helpful for adults to use to calm down and to assess their reactions to children's behaviors.

1. What was my inappropriate behavior?
2. Why was it inappropriate?
3. What was the reason for my behavior?
4. Why did I choose to behave this way?
5. Did my behavior help me achieve my purpose?
6. Why do I think so?
7. What are our shared home/classroom/school values?
8. How was my behavior not aligned with our values?
9. How did my behavior affect others?
10. How have others reacted to me?
11. How have I reacted to others?
12. How do they feel right now?
13. Why do I think so?
14. How could I change my reaction next time?
15. How could I affect the reaction of others next time?
16. How do I feel right now?
17. How do I want to feel?
18. What will I do right now?

TOOL 3.2

Tips for Active Listening

This is a list of tips that you could practice with your children and students to improve your active and attentive listening skills. Listening could be done at different levels, but when we are listening actively and attentively to others, we are giving others our undivided attention, and focusing on the other, seeking to understand them. This is called active, deep or attentive listening. When we are listening to our children or students, we need to let them know that we are truly attentive to what they are saying.

Tips for Active Listening
Non-Verbal

Smile
This makes the speaker feel heard, happy and in agreement.

Nod
This makes the speaker feel understood.

Facial Expressions
When you mimic the speaker's facial expressions, you show empathy.

Eye Contact
This makes the speaker feel respected and heard. However, certain cultures might read that differently. Also, shy speakers might feel intimidated. So, combine smiles and nods to encourage shy speakers.

Posture
Lean slightly forward or slightly sideways.

Refrain from Distractions
Refrain from looking at the clock, working on your computer, taking notes, or fidgeting because these behaviors give the message that you are not interested in what the speaker is saying.

Tips for Active Listening
Verbal

Summarize
Reiterate what you heard the speaker say, by briefly repeating the main ideas of what the speaker said.

Child: My friend does not want to play with me anymore. She is so mean.
You: You feel your friend is being mean because she does not want to play with you anymore?

Paraphrase
Say what the speaker said but in slightly different words.

Child: My friend does not want to play with me anymore. She is so mean.
You: You feel your friend is not being friendly with you?

Clarify
Ask questions to make sure you have understood what the speaker said. This also helps you be a better guide for your child to help them figure out what choices should be made next.

Child: My friend does not want to play with me anymore. She is so mean.
You: It does not feel good to be left out. Did she tell you that she does not want to play with you?

Reflect
Paraphrase or summarize what the speaker said, but include what you think the speaker is feeling.

Child: My friend does not want to play with me anymore. She is so mean.
You: You sound hurt because your friend does not want to play with you. I would be hurt, too, if my friend didn't want to play with me.

TOOL 3.3

Three-in-One Strategy

for Building Strong Relationships

At school, write down the names of your students, or use the class roster. Every day, choose three students to chat with before or after class, or during recess or dismissal. After you get the chance to chat with every student, go back and repeat the process. You could use the following as guiding questions, or you could come up with your own. Remember to ask follow up questions, too.

1. How is your day going so far?

2. How was your evening? Did you do anything special?

3. How was your weekend?

4. What plans do you have for next weekend?

5. Are you planning to do anything special after school today?

6. How was your game last night (if you know that they are part of a sports team)?

7. How are you doing with homework and projects?

8. How is your year going so far?

9. Are you enjoying your classes this term?

10. What projects are you working on?

11. What's your favorite class/project so far?

12. Have you made any new friends this year?

13. Are you enjoying my class this year?

14. Is there anything that you find particularly interesting/ difficult in our class this year?

15. How did you style your hair this way? I like it and would like to have the same hairdo.

TOOL 3.4

Daily Dose Strategy

for Building Strong Relationships

At home, spend uninterrupted time with your children every day to chat about anything they want. Spend at least twenty minutes every day with every child. You could use the following as guiding questions, or you could come up with your own. Remember to ask follow up questions, too.

1. How was your day today?

2. Anything special happened today?

3. Did you learn anything interesting today?

4. Did you experience anything upsetting today?

5. What plans do you have for tomorrow?

6. What do you enjoy doing most?

7. What activities would you like us to do together?

8. Let's name some positive things that happened to us today.

9. Let's name the blessings that we have.

10. Who is your best friend? Why are you best friends?

11. What do you want us to do next weekend/holiday?

12. Is there anything you want to improve in yourself? Why? How?

13. Do you have any special interests that you would like to focus on?

14. Is there anything in particular that is bothering you?

15. What do you plan to do to improve your situation?

Chapter Four
PLAN YOUR PRIORITIES

Decide on what truly matters in your life.
This is how you can live purposefully, not randomly.
Satisfaction with your life doesn't just happen;
you should plan for it.

What values are the most meaningful for you?

What values would you like to be dominant

in your home, classroom and school?

What specific behaviors exemplify your core values?

What positive behaviors do you want to teach others?

How willing are you to commit to your values?

So, by now, you have reflected on your own beliefs and attitudes, learned how to listen to your inner voice, tapped into your inner spring of heartfelt positivity, learned how to generate more positive emotions necessary for the well-being of yourself and your children, understood the essential elements of connecting strongly with them and learned how to strengthen those bonds. Now it is time to plan what you need to teach them.

What are the behavior expectations that you would like your children to exhibit? Think about the values in your home, school and community. What are the beliefs and principles that matter the most? What kind of future lifelong citizens do you want your children to be like? Does religion play a major role, or is it social and civil norms that govern? Whatever the religion or doctrines that govern your home, class or school, they all revolve around the same universal values: respect, responsibility, compassion, love, trust, and safety among many, many others.

When planning what behaviors you would like to see in your children, think about the values you would like to instill. Choose three to five values that are the most meaningful for your family, classroom or school environment. What do you want to focus on when educating your children? Is it teaching the importance of respect for others? Is it fostering the love for oneself and others? Does responsibility count as a fundamental value that you must develop in children? Does safety count as a priority that must be addressed? Think about all the values you were raised to believe, and consider others that are essential for humans to live in peaceful societies. How important is trust for you? Do you need to encourage cooperation for people to be more helpful and compassionate?

In the tool section, there is a non-exhaustive list of values for you to take a look at and select what matters most for you, your home, classroom and school.

In my experience as a parent, educator, coach and trainer, no matter what values you select, when aligning the specific behaviors that you expect from your children to these values, they all end up speaking a similar behavioral language.

So go ahead and select your main values. You could have a set of values pertinent to your home life, and another (or the same one) for your classroom and school. Use the activity in the Tool section to help you choose your core values.

After choosing your values, you need to decide on the specific observable behaviors that align with each value. Remember, the behaviors must be stated positively, i.e. they should state what the behavior should look like. For example, aligned with the value of RESPECT, a home rule could be: "I will use kind words when speaking with my brother." It should not be phrased negatively like this: "I will not insult my brother". We need to focus on what the children should do, not what they shouldn't do.

A behavioral example aligned with RESPECT in the classroom could be: "I will raise my hand for permission to speak." It is phrased positively and states what the children are expected to do. A negative statement, which we want to avoid, would be: "I will not blurt out answers." When we teach children a negative statement, it sticks to their head, and all they would think about would be the undesirable behavior. When we teach a positively stated behavior, the desirable behavior is what will resonate in their heads.

When statements are stated positively, not only will children know what behaviors are expected of them, they will also feel more motivated to follow them. Positive statements ignite good feelings of hope and enthusiasm in our brain that spread to the rest of our body.

Our brain will decipher every word we give it and will create the imagery associated with the message. If we want to see desirable behavior in our children, we should communicate this desirable behavior, not anything else.

Try this other exercise. Close your eyes and say:

I will help a needy person.

What do you feel? Do you feel the motivation to actually help a needy person when you come across one? Do you feel like a good person? Or, do you feel ashamed that you do not help needy people?

Now, close your eyes and say:

I will ignore the next needy person I see.

How does that make you feel? Do you feel like a good person following this instruction, or do you feel like a bad person? Do you feel triumphant for ignoring a needy person, or do you feel shame?

Positive statements light up positive emotions in our brain that spread through our bodily system. Negative statements impose negative feelings that we also feel throughout our body.

When I conduct school-wide evaluations, I interview students and try to find out, from them, what the expected behaviors are. Many of the responses I get are phrased negatively, "Do not run," or "Do not litter," or "Do not disrespect the teacher." When expectations are phrased negatively, students end up thinking about the negative or undesirable behavior, so that might be what they will actually do. Also, when the behavior expectations are general, "Respect the teacher," the students will not know how that looks. Moreover, should respecting the teacher be the only expectation? Or should students and teachers also be expected to respect each other? Think about what behaviors you would like to see in your children and students.

Try asking your son or daughter about the rules at home. You might be surprised with what they have to say. My friends who are new to the positive approach in teaching behavior, asked their son what the expected behaviors in their family were. His response, after a long pause, was, "I should not hit my brother. I should not keep my toys lying around. I should not answer back to my parents when they tell me to do something." They are all stated negatively. How can the child know what behavior is *expected* from him if he can only state what he is expected not to do?

In my family, my husband and I provide positive support, and we teach expected behaviors to our children. My friends decided to ask my children about what the rules were in our family. My little one, seven years at the time, responded, "I should use kind words with others." "I should follow my parents' instructions from the first time." "I should help others when they need my help." My friends were dumbfounded. Go ahead and try it with your children or students. Find out what they know in order to figure out what modifications you need to make to their teaching. Find out what behaviors they have already learned, and figure out what positive behaviors you need to teach them.

Now that you know how rules and expected behaviors should be phrased, what is the best way to come up with them? The best way is to generate them as a team. In your home, gather yourselves as parents or legal guardians together with the children. In the classroom, allocate time specific for rule generation. At the school building level, establish a team which has representation from different grade levels, subject areas, specializations, and administrative positions. In this case, the entire team would work together to select the values prior to generating the specific rules.

Let's say a parent, couple, teacher, or leadership team chose the values of respect, honesty, safety, kindness, and responsibility to promote in their home, class or school environment. The next step would be to gather the children, students, or team members and begin generating the specific behaviors that would demonstrate these values. Create a matrix, and write down the values on one side and align the specific behaviors that characterize these values. For example, to show the value of LOVE at home during morning routine, the specific behaviors that are aligned with LOVE could be: 'I say good morning to everyone; I wake up feeling grateful'.

Within the home environment, include every activity possible when deciding what the specific behavior expectations are. For example, in the matrix, include areas or activities that you would need to describe behaviors in, such as meal times, getting ready for school, homework routines, bedtime routines, family trips, travels, car rides, etc. Label any place where you would anticipate a learning process for expected behaviors, in order to avoid any confusion or misbehavior. Phrasing the behaviors in an observable and positive way allows children to know exactly what is expected of them. At the end of this chapter, there is an example of a behavior matrix for the home under Tool 4.2.

For the classroom environment, make a list of every activity and transition you would normally have in the classroom. Also, include activities outside of the classroom such as field trips or visits to the library. Then, define the behaviors that are expected in those activities. For example, what are the expected student behaviors during independent reading time, during group activities, when they need to ask for help, when they need to use the toilet, when they need to sharpen their pencil, when they arrive late, when they are doing a test, when they enter or leave the class? Brainstorm every possible activity and define the expected behaviors during those procedures and routines. Remember to define the behaviors in an observable and positive way. At the end of this chapter, there is an example of a behavior matrix for the classroom under Tool 4.3.

As for the school environment, get together as a team and make a list of all the common areas in the school that students could ever be in: the playground, hallways, cafeteria, library, dismissal area, nurse's station, etc. Begin deciding what the specific behavior expectations should look like in each of the areas. Define them and write them down in a matrix. This process might take time because you want to make sure that you have addressed every value you have chosen, and defined every behavior in an observable and positive way. At the end of this chapter, there is an example of a behavior matrix for the school under Tool 4.4.

TOOL 4.1

This is a tool that contains a non-exhaustive list of core values that I have selected from a very long list. As a family, class group, or team representative of a school, look at the values and think about which ones are the most important to you. Which ones reflect your core values and beliefs? These will be the factors that drive your behaviors and decisions. Choose three to five core values which are the most meaningful for you all. To help you pick these core values, begin by eliminating (crossing out) five, then another five, then another five, and so on, until you are left with five. Either keep those five, or pick the top three out of them.

VALUES			
Balance	Beauty	Accomplishment	Achievement
Tolerance	Citizenship	Health	Cooperation
Compassion	Creativity	Generosity	Determination
Courage	Faith	Fame	Friendship
Fun	Growth	Happiness	Honesty
Humor	Reliability	Inner Harmony	Justice
Kindness	Knowledge	Leadership	Punctuality
Love	Loyalty	Excellence	Openness
Optimism	Peace	Pleasure	Positivity
Popularity	Contentment	Religion	Family
Respect	Responsibility	Security	Honor
Gratitude	Perseverance	Stability	Success
Simplicity	Trustworthiness	Wealth	Wisdom
Adventure	Truthfulness	Safety	Learning
Integrity	Freedom	Acceptance	Spirituality

Now, to make sure that you all understand the meaning of the value you choose, each member will answer the questions below. This will allow every member to gain awareness into their beliefs and begin to set clear goals.

1. What does this value mean to me?

2. What does this value mean to us?

3. Why is this value important?

4. What should we do to show that we believe in this value of _____ (name the value)? Describe the specific behaviors aligned with this value.

5. How often should we show _____ (name the value)?

6. Name the areas and times for when we should behave this way.

TOOL 4.2

Behavior Matrix-AT HOME

Example

VALUES				
ROUTINE	**Responsibility**	**Perseverance**	**Health & Safety**	**Love**
Morning Routine	- I follow instructions	- I wake up on time & get ready for school	- I brush my teeth - I eat a healthy breakfast	- I wake up feeling grateful - I say good morning
Meal Time	- I eat all my food	- I finish my meals on time	- I make healthy choices - I wash my hands before and after	- I use good manners - I am thankful for the food
Play Time	- I report to an adult if I see an unsafe behavior	- I practice physical exercise	- I play safely	- I treat others kindly - I tidy up after I am done
Home-work	- I follow instructions	- I work hard	- I sit in a proper position	- I do my best work
Road Trip	- I respect nature - I keep my surroundings clean	- I am patient	- I buckle my seat belt - I keep my hands and feet in the car & to myself	- I admire my surroundings
Family Time	- I interact positively	- I actively participate in discussions	- I keep my hands and feet to myself	- I use kind words - I express my love - I help others
Bed Time	- I pack my school bag - I follow instructions - I sleep on time	- I read daily	- I take a bath - I brush my teeth - I sleep on time	- I wish everybody a good night - I count my blessings

TOOL 4.3

Behavior Matrix-IN THE CLASSROOM

Example

ROUTINE	Safety	Responsibility	Respect
		VALUES	
Independent Work	- I keep my hands and feet to myself - I use materials or equipment appropriately	- I follow instructions - I complete my work	- I use voice level 0-1 - I raise my hand to ask for help
Group Work	- I keep my hands and feet to myself - I use materials or equipment appropriately	- I do the work I am assigned to do - I actively participate	- I use voice level 1-2 - I listen while others speak - I show kindness to others - I work cooperatively
Test-Taking	- I stay in my place	- I do my best - I keep my eyes on my own work	- I use voice level 0 - I raise my hand to ask for help
Transitions	- I keep my hands and feet to myself - I walk	- I keep my place and classroom clean - I arrive on time to class	- I follow instructions
Bathroom Break	- I wash my hands after using the toilet - I keep my feet on the floor - I keep water in the sink	- I flush the toilet when I'm done - I go straight to the bathroom and back - I report problems to an adult	- I use voice level 0-1 - I respect the privacy of others - I knock on the stall door
Collecting/ Submitting	- I take care of property - I walk	- I follow instructions	- I wait for my turn - I use kind words

Voice Level Key: Level 0=Silence; Level 1=Whisper;
Level 2=Normal Talking; Level 3=Loud voice

TOOL 4.4

Behavior Matrix-AT SCHOOL

Example

ROUTINE	Safety	VALUES		
		Responsibility	Respect	
Hallway	- I walk - I keep my bag on my back - I keep my hands and feet to myself	- I go directly to where I need to be	- I use voice level 0-1 - I keep the hallways clean - I treat others kindly	
Playground	- I stay within the boundaries - I play safely	- I line up at the signal - I report problems to an adult	- I use voice level 2-3 - I keep the area clean - I treat others kindly	
Cafeteria	- I eat my own food - I wait patiently in line - I sit down and eat my food	- I make healthy choices	- I use voice level 2 - I wait in line for my turn - I say 'Please' and 'Thank you'. - I use good table manners	
Bus	- I remain in my seat with my back to the back of the seat - I keep my feet on the floor - I keep my hands to myself	- I get on and off the bus carefully	- I use voice level 2 - I treat others kindly	
Assembly	- I remain in my place	- I follow instructions	- I use voice level 0 - I am a positive role model	
Library	- I walk when finding a book	- I return books on time	- I treat books with care	

Voice Level Key: Level 0=Silence; Level 1=Whisper;
Level 2=Normal Talking; Level 3=Loud voice

Chapter Five
LEAD THE LEARNING
THROUGH DIRECT TEACHING

Our children come into the world unequipped. It is our duty, as parents and
educators, to purposefully teach them everything we expect them to know.

How patient do you think you will be as your children
gradually learn the expected behaviors?
Will you encourage them to keep trying even if they fail to
behave correctly the first time?
How will you teach, reteach, review and reinforce
the behavior expectations?
How often will you teach them?
What are your expectations for this process?
Do you consider this process challenging?
If you do, what do you need to be more prepared
to teach the expected behaviors?

You know what values are the most meaningful for you, you have described the specific behaviors, aligned them with the values, and you have stated them positively. Now what?

Now that you know the 'what' and have reflected on the 'why', you need to figure out the 'how' and the 'when'.

I have interviewed many teachers from many schools over the years, and most of them seem to be skillful at deciding on what they expect children to do and not to do. They create colorful and wordy posters and hang them up in their classrooms and schools. Parents might hang picture frames on their house walls of sayings or proverbs that communicate expected behaviors. But, what then? Is it an expectation by the adults that children will know how to behave because there are posters and picture frames hanging on the walls?

Let me tell you something: I have passed by certain walls and streets dozens of times, but never paid attention to what was hanging there. Does that mean that I should know what there is, because I have passed by the same spot dozens of times? No. If I don't consciously make an effort, or if someone does not consciously direct me to them, I would fail to notice a lot of things. If children are not explicitly taught the expected behaviors, they might not notice the poster that explains the rules. The probability is very high that the children will not decide to self-teach themselves the rules. Someone needs to point them out and purposefully teach them.

So, you have decided on the values that matter to you the most, and—as a family, class or team—decided on the specific behaviors that would imply that the values are being acted upon. Now, you need to explicitly teach them.

Teaching the rules has to be done directly and explicitly. Like I said before, we cannot hang a poster of rules on the wall and expect that students will follow them. Do math teachers do that when they teach a new math concept? Do they hang a poster with the rule on the wall, and expect students to learn it, understand and apply it? Of course not. When a math teacher teaches a new skill, they follow steps to teach it, give plenty of examples, and allow children to practice it.

It should be the same when teaching the expected behaviors. Do parents expect their children to get in the car and buckle up their seat belts so that they are safe? This would be ideal. But what if the children forget? Shouldn't parents explicitly teach the importance of putting the seat belt on in order to be safe, show their children how it is done, remind them, and acknowledge when they remember to buckle up?

My children remember to buckle their seat belts almost every time, but there are still times when they might forget. My role is to remind them gently every time we get in the car. I do it whenever we get in the car, by saying, "Remember to say READY when your seat belts are buckled!" This reminds them—if they have forgotten—that they need to buckle up.

What is my aim as a driving parent? Is it for my children to be safe, or do I want to wait for them to forget so I could get angry with them? What is my goal? What is their goal? To be safe. So, let's focus on being safe and provide all the support that is required.

What about in class? What is my goal for my students? For them to be successful, or for them to get punished? If I aim for them to be successful, I need to help them by setting up the foundation for their success, through positive, proactive and preventive practices—teaching them the necessary behaviors, reminding them and praising their efforts.

Some teachers that I had interviewed in schools when I conducted school-wide assessments expressed how they were disturbed by all the behavior problems in their classroom. My question was straight to the point, "Do you teach the rules?" The majority of responses were, "Well, yes, of course! I taught the rules in September!" But, the problem was that it was April when I conducted the interviews. Is it enough to teach the rules in September, and then expect that students know what is expected of them in April? When you teach a math concept in September, do you think students will continue to master it in April? They will if you constantly review, reteach and practice it, while providing regular feedback. Think about how often you need to teach and reteach expected behaviors.

A good solid initial teaching process is a must. Initially, you need to allocate enough time daily to teach the behaviors. At home, it could be every evening before going to bed, or in the morning before getting ready for school, or even during family meal times or right after. You and your family members could gather together and talk about behavior expectations. Figure out what time works best for you as a family. I personally prefer the evening time, when the pace is slower and there is no rush to get ready for school or activities. We can all focus and be ready to listen and learn.

Take the time at home to teach the behaviors. Then, use the opportunity of when you are actually in an activity (such as meal times, in the car, in the airport, etc.) to reteach the behaviors in the natural context.

When introducing the new behaviors you would like to teach in the classroom, teach them, explicitly, for an entire week or two. After that, review them every week right after the weekend. It should only take a few minutes from your lesson time. This should set your students up for success. You would have laid the foundation for their readiness to follow the behavior expectations, and avoided any situations where students might forget what is expected of them.

Visuals for the expected behaviors and rules are very helpful aids to refer to as you teach the behaviors. I see a lot of rules on posters in school common areas, but sometimes they are too wordy. Many classrooms I have seen do not have rules posted. If there are, they are not aligned to common values shared across the school. It seems that in many schools, rules are either non-existent, too wordy and illegible, or not aligned to a set of shared school-wide values. This just leads to confusion. Use these visuals as support to point out to when teaching and re-teaching the expectations. Using visuals is more powerful than just speaking about the expected behaviors.

When you teach the behavior expectations, do that one behavior at a time. After the initial and thorough teaching, the best follow-up would be to teach them as they happen. For example, before giving students an independent task, teach them what behaviors they are expected to demonstrate to show that they are following expectations. Include procedures for things like if they need your help, want to ask a question, or need to throw something in the rubbish bin. Teach every single procedure prior to beginning. Praise students who are following expectations, and support others who forget. Tell them that they will eventually become proficient, and encourage them to follow expectations.

Another important activity is to give examples and non-examples of correct behaviors. This could be a fun activity that will motivate them to behave well. After the first two weeks, a simple reminder right before the activity should be enough for students to know what they are expected to behave like.

In the classroom, a teacher could spend some time before beginning the lesson, and teach the behaviors. Just as the teacher would create interesting visuals to teach a lesson, the same could be done to teach behaviors. Remember: good teaching includes examples and non-examples, so don't forget to provide those examples and role modeling opportunities.

After the initial teaching and follow-up, when do you think you should review and reteach? Every week right after the weekend? Every day right before the lesson? After holidays?

The answer is, "All of the above."

When students come back after the weekend, they need to be reminded.

Another important approach is right before any lesson or activity. After you give instructions for the students to get started with a certain activity, sometimes students take advantage of the opportunity to be left alone to make choices, and they might make wrong, undesirable choices. 'Catch' them right before they do so and set them up for success.

For example, when you give instructions for an independent task, right before you say "GO", review the behavior expectations for that task, like this: "Remember! Raise your hand if you need help. Voice level during independent activities is ONE. Focus on the task you are working on. Complete it in the allotted time. You may leave your seat to get materials, and you need to go straight back when you get what you need. I will come around and give points to all of you who are on task and I will help you if you need anything." This way, you have laid the foundation for all of them to follow expectations and you have set them up for success. How long did it take? Just a few seconds, but it would save you a lot of time from having to redirect and remind individual students later on if they are not following expectations.

Do you notice how every time you are on the plane, getting ready for take-off, they begin their routine lesson of what you should do in case of an emergency and that smoking on board the plane is strictly prohibited? I have been on various airlines and listened to this routine hundreds of times already and in more languages than you could imagine. So why don't they just ask us if we have been through the drill before, to save us the time of having to listen to it again? The reason is, they want to be as proactive and preventive as possible to avoid any confusion, in case any emergency were to happen or in case somebody decides to light up a cigarette. They teach the behavior expectations every time you board a plane, no matter how knowledgeable you are about the drill. It is a precautionary drill.

Do the same with your students and children. Teach them and remind them about the expected behaviors, every time, as a precautionary drill.

An example in the home environment could be homework routine. Let's say the homework routine is that your child is expected to come home from school, eat lunch and start with their homework. When your child is finishing off lunch, you could remind them by saying, "Remember! When you finish lunch, you should go straight to your room and begin working on your homework. I am here if you need any help. Just let me know. Remember to keep your phone off and away until you finish your homework. I know you will do the right thing. You are always responsible and you know what has to be done." You reminded them of what they are expected to do, and you threw in a positive and encouraging statement that will surely motivate them to do what they are supposed to be doing! Consider it a precautionary drill and a setup for success. I will talk more about positive interactions and encouragement in the next chapter.

What about teaching the behavior expectations of the school common areas? Remember in the last chapter, I discussed how a team would define the behaviors that are aligned to the school-wide values. These should be written down in a matrix that contains all the values, common areas and defined behaviors.

Next, a plan must be created for them to be taught to the students. This plan should include a joint effort among the entire school staff. The team could create simple plans for teaching the behaviors in every common area, and create a schedule for the teachers and support staff to know when they will be teaching these behaviors.

First, a schedule should be created for the entire school for the period of at least two weeks. Every day, teachers would know which behaviors for which common areas they are expected to teach their students. A plan like this helps avoid redundancy, and commits the entire school staff to delivering the lessons to the students.

Following this plan, a schedule must be created to reteach and review the behavior expectations in the common areas regularly throughout the year. The schedule must take into consideration the first day after the weekend, and the first week after every holiday. When I was a teacher, I worked with other grade level teachers to deliver behavior expectations review sessions for our grade level students when we felt they needed to be retaught and reminded. Monthly student assemblies are also excellent opportunities to review behavior expectations. Use every opportunity to remind your students. Remember, our role is to help them succeed, not fail.

One of the many incidents that I remember fills my heart with admiration. When I was a teacher, I was very consistent when teaching my students classroom expectations, routines and procedures. One time, I had informed the school that I was going to be late because I had a meeting at my son's school. So, I had asked for coverage for my seventh grade class for the first two periods. What happened was that just one of my classes had been covered by a substitute teacher; the second was left with no teacher. I arrived to school fifteen minutes before the end of the second period reading class, and made my way into my classroom. I found my students sitting in their places, reading silently, writing in their journals, and chatting in a low voice (voice level 1).

I was surprised, firstly, because there was no teacher covering my class. But my surprise did not last for long, because I was so proud of them for following expectations, even without supervision! It was an expectation for students to come to reading class prepared, use voice level 1 (whisper) during independent activities, read silently, answer comprehension questions that were assigned during the previous class, and write in their journals in response to prompts that I had already added to their journals. They were doing all of that. Not one student was out of their seat, and no one was being foolish in any way. They were responsible, respectful and safe in every way—just like I had taught them to be. I was speechless. I acknowledged their behavior with plenty of praise. I even planned for a celebration for the following week— movie and pizza in the classroom during lunch time.

So how come they followed expectations when I was not there? Why didn't they—as many students might—abuse this opportunity of freedom to be goofy, play with their phones, socialize or possibly be reckless? Year after year, I was told that I had the 'easy class' and that I was lucky to have well-behaved students. Whenever I heard that, I smiled and agreed. But, that wasn't the truth. It wasn't that I was always blessed with the 'well-behaved' students. I was a teacher for more than ten years. Could I have been lucky every single time? No, of course not.

The reason why I had the 'good' kids was because I helped them behave well. I built strong relationships with them based on trust and respect. I taught them how they should behave and why they should be that way. I taught them that they were the ones who made their choices and that they were responsible for every choice they made. I showed them compassion and love. I demonstrated forgiveness and encouragement. I was merciful but systematic and consistent. I taught them the values of honor, respect, responsibility, compassion, safety and perseverance among many others. I defended them and asked for their cooperation. I expressed how much I loved them and how proud I was of them.

Go ahead. Reflect, listen, connect, plan and teach your children and students—then watch them become their best.

TOOL 5.1

The DIRECT Model for Teaching Behavior

Teaching must be purposeful, deliberate, conscious and explicit. This tool will guide you with the steps for teaching every behavior. Follow the six steps below:

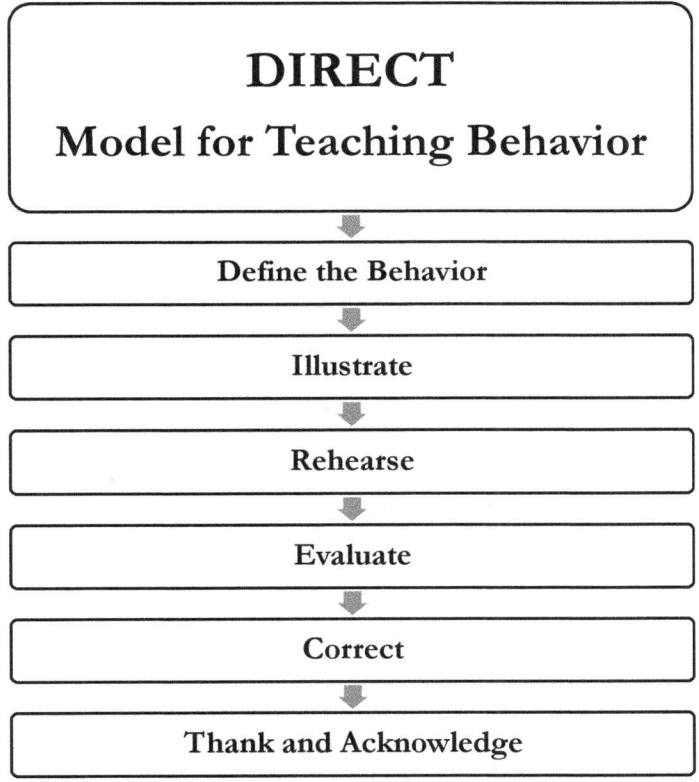

DIRECT

Model for Teaching Behavior

Define the Behavior

Illustrate

Rehearse

Evaluate

Correct

Thank and Acknowledge

1. Define the behavior you want to teach.

For the value of RESPECT in the home, you could say: "In the morning, when you wake up, you show respect by saying GOOD MORNING to your family members."

For the value of LOVE or GRATITUDE, you could say: "In the morning, when you wake up, you show Love and Gratitude by saying to yourself 'Thank you God for another day' to yourself."

For the value of RESPONSIBILTY in the classroom, you could say: "When you first enter the classroom, you show responsibility by putting your bag in your cubby, taking out your journal, and beginning with your entry task which is written on the board."

2. Illustrate by giving examples and by modeling the behavior.

At home, show that you are waking up and getting out of bed while saying:

"Good morning, everyone," when modeling the value of Respect.

"Thank you God for another day," when modeling the value of Gratitude.

Model the behavior in the classroom by showing that you are walking into the classroom, putting your bag in the cubby, taking out your journal, and beginning with your entry task, to show the value of Responsibility.

3. Rehearse together by giving examples and non-examples, and by giving practice opportunities.

Give examples and non-examples by saying:

Would you show Respect when waking up if you say: "Hey, get out of my face!"?

Would you show Respect when waking up if you say: "Good morning, my lovely family!"?

Would you show Gratitude when waking up if you say: "I hate waking up!"?

Would you show Gratitude when waking up if you say: "Thank you God for another beautiful day!"?

Would you show Responsibility when entering the classroom if you walk up to your friends and start chatting?

Would you show Responsibility when entering the classroom if you put your bag in place, take out your journal and begin your entry task?

Practice in the natural setting. This is fun for children and students and it also makes the learning more meaningful.

Go to your child's bedroom and have them practice getting out of bed and showing Respect or Gratitude.

Ask a few volunteers to practice entering the classroom and showing Responsibility.

4. **Evaluate by observing and monitoring the appropriate behavior.**

    Watch to see how well they are doing the next day and on future occasions.

5. **Correct and redirect to the desired behavior.**

    If they forget, correct their behavior by reminding them of the expected behavior.

    "Remember that we need to show respect to each other by saying 'Good morning' to each other when we wake up. Could you please say Good morning to show how respectful you are?"

    "Remember that we would like to show our Gratitude to God for blessing us with another day. Could you please try harder to thank God for blessing us with another day?"

    "Remember that you need to show Responsibility when you enter the classroom by putting your bag in your cubby, getting your journal out and beginning with your task."

    When they correct their behavior, acknowledge immediately! Praise them and show your appreciation for their efforts.

6. **Thank and acknowledge their behavior when they behave the right way by praising and giving specific feedback about what they did right and how well they did.**

    "It's so beautiful to hear your GOOD MORNINGS. Thank you for being Respectful."

"You do such a great job thanking God for another blessed day. Thank you for being Grateful!"

"You did a wonderful job of entering the classroom, putting your bag away and beginning with your work. You are so Responsible."

These steps should be followed for every behavior you teach.

Chapter Six
EMPOWER THROUGH ACKNOWLEDGEMENT

How we interact with our children

affects how they interact with the world.

If you want a better world, interact positively.

Do you believe in positive interactions with children?

What kinds of interactions are you comfortable with?

How do you see yourself encouraging children to behave well?

Do you know how to praise children?

What kind of rewards do you see yourself giving?

**Do you know how to give specific
positive feedback to children?**

What kind of attention do you see yourself giving children?

**Do you feel that you tend to point out incorrect
behaviors in children quite frequently?**

**Do you feel you should interact with children
more positively than negatively?**

What kind of interactions from adults were you
accustomed to while growing up?
Are you ready to behave differently with your
children as compared to how you were raised?
What do you honestly feel towards your children?
Are you ready to acknowledge their positive behaviors?
Are you ready to catch them being good?

Children need to know from us if they have done
something right or wrong. It is our duty to provide specific
feedback about what they have done. This is the only way they will
learn what they did right or what they did wrong. Acknowledging
child behavior includes the positive interactions you have with the
children.

Interactions with children could be verbal, nonverbal or
tangible. My advice is for you to focus more on the first two, and
not to overuse the tangible methods. We would like to encourage
children and students to feel intrinsically rewarded, and not only
rely on external rewards for acknowledgment.

Ask yourself this: Do my children/students only behave
well when I give out a tangible reward? Or, do I see sparkles in their
eyes when I express how proud I am of their behavior? Tangibles
are necessary because they remind us, as adults, to acknowledge
desirable behavior; and they are also a good culmination of student
efforts to follow behavior expectations. But, the actual reward itself
should not be the focus. The verbal and nonverbal positive

interactions should matter more and should be encouraged the most.

I asked my thirteen-year-old son once, "What is the most motivating reward (monetary or non-monetary) that you would like to receive from us, your parents?"

His response to me was: "For you to say that you were proud of me."

Positive and meaningful interactions with children touch their core and stimulate them to behave well. The tangible reward is an added by-product, but not as essential as verbally acknowledging their positive behavior.

How many students or children do you know who often get gifts and presents for successes? How many of them exhibit good behavior and are intrinsically motivated to behave well? Not many of them.

Our aim as adults is to develop a more sophisticated level of morality in our children – future citizens who will behave well because it feels good, not because they will be given a prize for that. We hope that we can raise citizens that will be socially responsible because it is the right thing to do, and not because they anticipate a reward or are afraid of punishment.

Verbal acknowledgment includes praise, giving specific positive feedback, and providing contingent and non-contingent attention.

Let's first look at praise. How many of us smile, feel proud and happy when we receive praise from our supervisor at work? How positive do we feel when we hear a positive remark that praises our efforts and dedication? We feel terrific, right? Why would children be any different? Watch their faces when you praise them. Their eyes light up and their lips purse in a smile of satisfaction. When you praise them, you are tapping into their well of positive emotions, allowing the feelings to surmount and conquer their minds and hearts. Their brains will be inclined to behave well again and again because they felt good as a result the first time.

A mistake that some parents and educators make, however, is to praise children for the sake of praising, and not for the sake of acknowledging and reinforcing the desired behavior. I have observed classes where students gave the teacher a hard time, did not finish their work and did not follow the expected behaviors for the task they were asked to do. At the end of the lesson, when the bell rang, the teacher said, "Great job, guys!" Great job for what? For not following expectations? For giving her a hard time? For not finishing their work? The praise was not relevant and completely misleading.

During the post-conference, I asked the teacher, "You said, Great Job, guys. What was the great job you were praising?" The teacher's response was, "Well, they would normally not have done anything; but this time, they managed to complete the first section of the assignment. So I praised that."

My response was, "Do you think they understood what it was you were praising?" She had no answer.

An example of what could have been said was, "Great job for completing the first half of the assignment. You guys are making good progress. Let's remember next time to follow classroom expectations and work using voice level ONE, focusing on our work to get it all done, and to raise our hands if we need help."

The praise in this example is specific to what they actually did well, and that is a valuable learning opportunity for the students to know what they did well and what behavior needs to be repeated.

The statements after that were reminders for the students to be ready and to follow expectations. They are also a form of specific feedback telling them that they were not on-task nor did they behave very well, but that the teacher truly believes that they are capable of following expectations. These statements give out the message of hope and encouragement. When children feel hopeful that adults believe in them, they are motivated to behave well.

This example also showed how we can give specific positive feedback. When we give feedback, we are explaining to children what they did right or wrong. We, as parents and educators, should provide feedback for children to know if they have learned a skill or not. If I ask an addition question and a student gives a wrong answer, I correct their answer and explain where they went wrong in the calculation. This feedback helps them learn how to do it right the next time. When children give the right answer, the feedback we provide is something like, "Yes. That is the right answer." We were specific in telling the student that their answer was correct. It is the same with behavior.

When a child raises her hand to answer, praise and give specific feedback about their behavior by acknowledging what they did right, "Great job for raising your hand to take a turn!" You will notice how she smiles, and how others will want to do the same to receive the same praise with the specific positive feedback.

Another student might begin writing on their task, as instructed to do so, so you could say, "You have very neat handwriting and you remembered to write after the margin." Or, with another student, you could say, "You started working on the assignment as soon as I said GO. This shows how responsible you are to get your work done." This is specific, positive feedback that will make the students proud of their behaviors and achievements, and will be a learning opportunity for them to know that it is an expectation to use neat handwriting, to write after the margin, and to begin work immediately.

Make your feedback as specific as possible. It is part of your ongoing assessments that allow you to assess student learning—behavior included! Isn't your role as a teacher to assess student learning in an ongoing fashion? Reinforce positive student behaviors to teach students what they did right, and to encourage the behavior to occur again.

Parents have a role to let their children know what they are doing right, too. Whenever my children follow instructions the first time, I provide specific positive feedback by saying, "You followed instructions the first time I gave it. You are showing that you know how to do the right thing." Watch them smile when I say it! They also add a, "Thank you, mommy," to show their appreciation.

One time, my son rushed back home when a fight began in our residential compound, and he told me about it. I responded with specific positive feedback to let him know that he did the right thing by reporting the incident to an adult, and by being proactive to avoid the possibility of a gruesome ending to a fight.

My response was, "You rushed back home immediately when the fight broke out to let me—the adult—know what is happening so I can interfere and stop the fight before it grows and before somebody gets hurt. This is a responsible thing to do. I will rush outside and intervene right now!" Or, you could provide the feedback after you intervene to stop the fight, depending on how serious the problem is.

I acknowledged how responsible my son was, and provided the specific feedback that will teach him that he did the right thing by reporting to an adult immediately at the onset of the fight. This kind of responsible behavior will definitely be repeated in similar future incidents.

Another form of verbal acknowledgement is providing contingent and non-contingent attention. Children thrive on attention. The message they get when adults provide attention, is that we care about them. We care enough to give attention to the work they are doing, and we care enough to give attention to them as individuals with interests, unique personalities and characters.

Contingent attention is when you provide attention to something they are doing that they are supposed to be doing. For example, if my son is doing his homework (and he is supposed to be doing his homework because that is the daily homework routine), I could pass by his room and look at his work and show interest in the assignment that he is doing. This attention is encouraging for him because it allows him to share what he is learning with me and to show me his work that he is proud of completing independently.

It is the same in the classroom. Show an interest in your students' work. When they are working, go around and interact with them about their work. It is motivating for them and also shows them that they have your support. Don't just go and sit behind your desk.

Non-contingent attention is when you provide attention that is not tied to a specific action of theirs. So, your attention will not have anything to do with their specific work or behavior, but rather with their personalities and outside interests. Find out what your students do in their spare time, what clubs they go to, or what sports they practice. Strike up a brief conversation about that, either in the hallway, during recess, or as they enter the classroom. Be at the door when children walk in and greet them. Ask them how their day has been. Ask them about how their evening was or how they spent their weekend. These interactions send the message that you admire them as individuals, that you genuinely care about them, and that you are not there only to deliver subject matter. This motivates children and builds strong relationships with them.

At home, how much time do you spend talking to your children about their interests and how their day went? Is your day so busy with feeding, dropping off to school and activities, helping with homework and rushing them to wash and get to bed? How much of that time do you spend talking with them about what they did during the day? How often do you ask them what they enjoy doing over the weekend, or what their favorite game was, or how they enjoyed their trip to the beach with you?

My children have different bedtimes because of the age difference, so I spend separate times with each child every night. My youngest can easily express his thoughts about anything we decide to discuss during our private time together. He communicates what he did during his afternoon play time and what he is looking forward to. The attention I provide him sends him the message that I care about him, about his interests, and that I would like to be involved. He voices out what he expects of me too, which is valuable feedback for me as a parent. We need to listen to our children's needs if we expect ourselves to cater to them.

As for my eldest, who is a teenager now, he also enjoys telling me about his interests, thoughts and feelings during our private time every evening. He also voices out his teenage concerns and asks me for advice. This relationship building practice is remarkably powerful. It tells our children that they are not alone, that we are here to help and support them, that we care enough to listen, and that what they say is important.

I look at so many families with children who give them a hard time with defiance and disobedience. Do these parents take the time to build their relationships with their children? Do they show their children that they love them unconditionally? Do they clearly communicate to their children that they are interested in them and in their likes and dislikes? Is it only an expectation that your children should know that you care about them and that you are there for them, or do you explicitly tell them and show them by spending time with them and providing the attention that they seek?

A lot of times, the function of student behavior is to seek attention from adults or from peers. How are you supporting your children in getting their needs met in the right way?

Think about your interactions with your children. Are you only focused on getting them fed, clothed and educated? Or do you take the time to develop the relationship between you that will help them grow in a magnitude of ways?

What about your students? Are you primarily concerned with getting them ready for exams and for your class average to reflect what an excellent teacher you are? Or do you take the time to build relationships with your students to make them stronger and happier individuals who are conscientious and ready for the future?

Acknowledgement can also be nonverbal. Nonverbal acknowledgement includes using body language and facial expressions to provide attention to desirable behavior and to help build the strong connections. When your students are on-task and engaged in their assignment, what do you do? Do you walk around the classroom, move close to students and give them a pat on the back or a thumbs up? Do you smile at them if they look up and see you standing next to them? These positive nonverbal acknowledgments are strong and effective enough to make your students feel good about working hard and doing what they are supposed to be doing.

What about your children at home? If you catch your daughter saying something kind to her sister, wouldn't a wink acknowledge that she said something kind to her sister, that you appreciate her kindness and are proud of her? Your wink would surely make her feel delighted that her behavior was kind to her sister. What about moving close to your children when they are playing responsibly in their room and giving them a hug? This reinforces their responsible play behavior and also tells them that you love them. Positive emotions will be tapped even more, flooding hearts and minds with joy and love.

One time while I was still at work, I received a phone call from the babysitter. My children normally arrive home before I do, and spend two hours with the babysitter before I get home. The babysitter was complaining that my eight year old did not want to practice his piano before the piano teacher arrived, so I asked to speak to him on the phone. Within seconds, my mind was deciding on the best way to handle this issue of defiance.

When I heard my son's voice, I said, "Hey! How are you? I hope you had a good day at school!" I felt he was about to complain about not wanting to practice the piano, so I continued with what I wanted to say immediately. "I just found out something wonderful!"

"What is it?" he said.

"I just checked Class Dojo and you have seven positives for being ready to learn and for working hard! Your behavior is always so impressive. Thank you for working hard at school and for being ready to learn!"

He was ecstatic!

"Yes! I worked really hard today!"

"Yes, I'm sure you did, as you always do." I could feel his lips smiling and his face lighting up. I wanted to catch this moment to move on to talk about practicing the piano quickly.

"Baby, I would like you to practice your piano for twenty minutes. The teacher is coming at half past four, and she would love to hear how well you are playing."

I did not finish my words when I heard the piano keys playing. It was magic!

I arrived home at four—forty five minutes after our phone call—and he was still playing!

Interacting positively with your children should become a habit—a culture. It's not about trying it once and saying that it did not work. It is about practicing it every day and in every instance, until it becomes a habit and dominates the way you all interact with each other. I know that some of you are saying that this is hard and requires a lot of effort. But, when you see how successful this will be in helping your children and students behave well, you will be motivated to proceed. It is really worth all the effort. Just do it!

I have heard from teachers that they tried, but it didn't work. They tried it once or twice, but that it was ineffective. It will not work if you are inconsistent with your interactions. You cannot interact negatively on most occasions and then expect that one positive interaction will fix it. It has to become your culture and an integral part of your daily habits.

Keep at it. Don't despair if you reprimand, scold, or react negatively to your children's misbehavior. Instead, make a deal with yourself that you will 'owe' them positive interactions for every negative one. The more positives to negatives you provide, the more you will counterbalance the negative effect. It is a simple ratio: for every negative interaction, you need to provide them with at least three positives.

For example, if you find yourself saying, "You should be doing your homework. Why haven't you started yet? Your phone should be off and away!" Counterbalance that by interacting positively the moment they begin with their homework, or even before that, by pointing out to something they have done well.

"Your room looks really tidy. I'm impressed that you cleaned it up so well. This will help create a better environment so you could begin with your homework." This will bring about positive feelings in them and encourage them to do something good so they could receive more positives from you. When they do manage to begin with their work, acknowledge by saying, "Good job beginning with your work. I always know that you will do the right thing."

So far, these are two positives to one negative. Try to find one more thing. You might want to check on them later and praise them for their neat work or for their diligence. You could continue the positive interactions by acknowledging something you heard that they did at school, or for a kind interaction with their sibling. Just keep interacting positively! Remember, if you do need to redirect them again, just remember that you 'owe' them positives in return. A pat on the back, a wink or hug also count as positives. So, go ahead and do it!

Finally, another form of acknowledgment includes tangible methods such as rewards, certificates, or points that add up to rewards. Even though verbal and nonverbal acknowledgment should be stressed more than tangible methods, the latter is nevertheless useful as a culmination of all the efforts that children are making to following behavior expectations. They are also a helpful reminder for us to remember to acknowledge students verbally as we hand out the reward.

Have children work hard for them; have them consistently display desired behavior before they arrive at tangible rewards. Make the culmination of consistent good behavior a celebration. Most importantly, remember to highlight the specific behavior that you are rewarding. Don't just hand out the reward. Remember: you are creating a culture of positive behavior that is rewarded through acknowledgement, NOT a culture of rewards. To help you create this culture, follow the PLP Model to verbally acknowledge behavior. If you are planning to give a reward, follow the steps in the PLP Model right before you hand out the reward.

At home, I give my children points for following behavior expectations. The rewards that they could earn are written in a list that they created with me. Whenever they gather a certain number of points, they could purchase any of the rewards in the list.

Just be mindful of the kinds of rewards you are agreeing on. Do not make most of the rewards 'toys'. Try to include things like 'movie night with mom and dad' or 'game night' or 'play day in the park' to really encourage the social connections.

TOOL 6.1 POSITIVE INTERACTIONS VINE

Every day, tally mark the number of times you practice any of these methods at home or at school.

Ask yourself: Am I satisfied with my performance? Do I aim to do the same or better tomorrow?

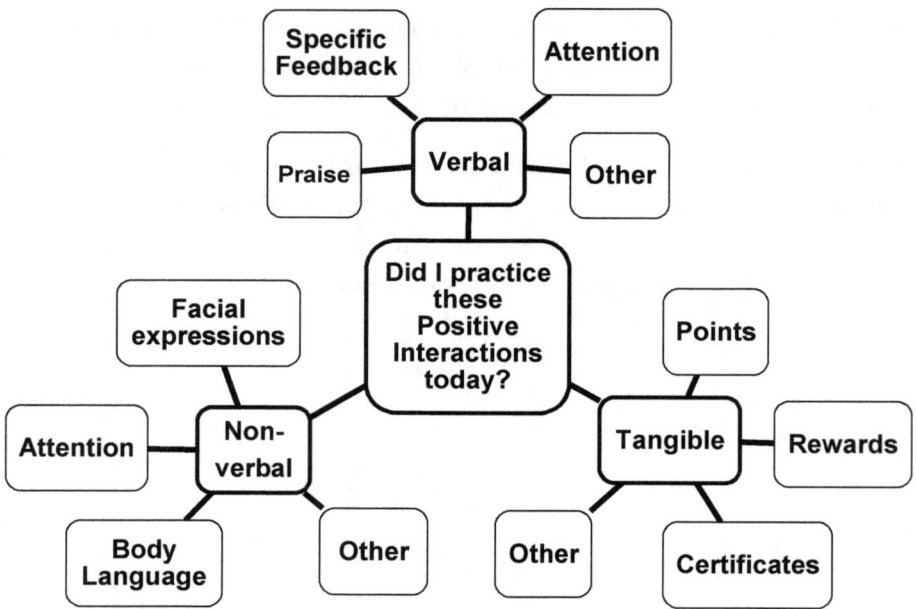

TOOL 6.2

My experience as a teacher, coach and leader in schools has shown me that many adults do not acknowledge desired child behavior not because they do not want to, but because they do not know how. It is very simple. I will give you a three step model for verbal acknowledgement that is easy to remember and implement every time your child or student behaves well. Most importantly, remember to follow it every time they follow expectations. This model strengthens the child's sense of pride for behaving well. It satiates their need for positive adult attention and develops their intrinsic motivation to behave well.

PLP Model to Verbally Acknowledge Behavior

1. POINT OUT the desirable behavior
2. LINK it to the values
3. PRAISE their efforts

PLP Model to Verbally Acknowledge Behavior

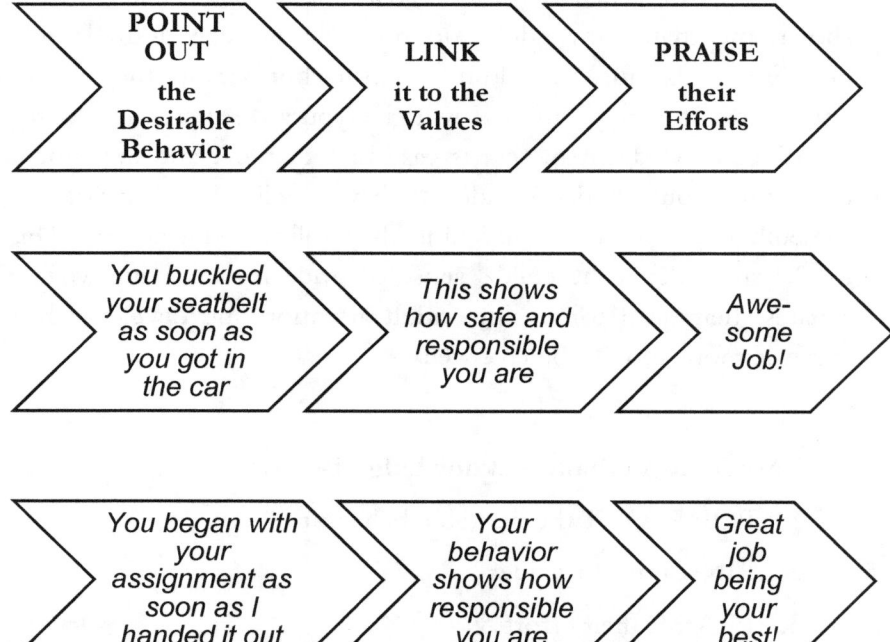

Chapter Seven
TACTFULLY CORRECT

Why should we make children feel bad if
our aim is for them to be good?

What does 'consequence' mean to you?

Are consequences an opportunity for you to punish?

Do you believe in punishment?

What kind of consequences did you experience as a child?

How have these consequences shaped you
and your behavior now?

Do you see consequences as an opportunity for you to teach
children to be accountable for their actions and choices?

How do you discuss consequences with children?

Are you consistent in implementing a consequence system?

What feelings do you experience
when implementing a consequence system?

Do you remain calm or do you express
your anger and irritation?

My eight-year-old son's schoolteacher contacted me last month to tell me that my son was involved in a fight with his peers. He explained the scenario, as well as what he, the teacher, did to handle the situation. What I did at home was to hold a conference with my son. First, I asked him what happened. Then, I asked him to think about how his behavioral choices affected others. We discussed other alternatives to how he could have behaved, that would not have led to a fight. This discussion contained feedback on his behavioral choices and their impact – most of which he came up with himself. It was a valuable learning opportunity for him to learn how to act the next time he is faced with a similar conflict.

The first thing we need to teach our children is that there are natural consequences to every choice we make, and that we must hold ourselves accountable for these choices. When children behave in a certain way, it is a choice they make. We, as adults, lay the foundation by teaching the expected behaviors through explicit teaching, modeling, reviewing, re-teaching, acknowledging, reinforcing, rewarding, celebrating and correcting. Within this process, children must learn that they have a choice to make: to follow behavior expectations or not. Every choice they make will lead to certain results. Just as we teach the behaviors, we must also teach the consequences. If they repeatedly fail to behave in a desirable way, we should follow a consequence system.

The system should begin with non-progressive consequences for early-stage corrections. These non-progressive consequences are adult behaviors that help redirect the child to the correct behavior. We want to avoid responding with a full-blown consequence that is not proportional with the misbehavior. We also do not want to jump to progressive consequences before we give the children a chance to fix their behavior and improve their choices. We need to help and support the child by giving reminders and prompts. Remember, your goal is to help children be successful. If reminders and prompts could do the trick of diverting them back to the right track, then let's do it. Refer to Tool 7.1 for a visual of the Non-Progressive Consequence System.

These non-progressive opportunities that help redirect children include verbal and nonverbal adult behaviors. Nonverbal prompts include prolonged eye contact or standing close to the child (proximity is effective). After that, we could give verbal prompts such as gentle verbal reminders to redirect the child to the correct behavior. Look at Tool 7.2 for a step by step explanation of the PLREP Model to Verbally Redirect Behavior.

Another method could be to ignore the child and instead, praise others who are behaving properly. If we find that the location of a child within a group or classroom setting is negatively influencing the child's behavior or causing a distraction, a good idea would be the modification of the setting, such as changing their seat.

When I was a teacher, I always intervened in the seating arrangement. Individual and group dynamics play a strong role in how ready and successful the students will be behaviorally. Sitting closer or farther away from the teacher, near a window or door, close to children that they are not on good terms with, are all dynamics to consider. Remember, we need to lay the foundation for children to be successful. Let's support them to be better and avoid creating traps that will lead them to misbehavior.

I am sure you practice a similar approach with your own children. How many times were you sitting in a restaurant and both of your children began arguing? With my children, a lot of times. What would be a non-progressive consequence that you would follow? Change their seating arrangement or give them a distracting activity to do. Result? The arguments stop. I could jump to punishment and have them miss out on something they are looking forward to. But, why should I do that? Do I want their behavior to change and improve, or do I want to make them feel bad and discouraged? If I punish them, they might hate me or resent each other, and they could find a way to retaliate. What is my goal? What do I want them to learn? How do I want to spend my family meal time in the restaurant? Do I want them to be successful and well-behaved, or do I want them to suffer because they are arguing and they know they should be kind to each other?

The moment my children are behaving well, and possibly interacting well with each other, I could catch them being good and give specific positive feedback and praise to acknowledge their behavior. "I admire how you are speaking to each other and playing kindly with one another. I love seeing the brotherly love between you. Thank you for making today an enjoyable family day out!" You can be sure that they will continue with their positive interactions. If they do however forget, and get into another squabble, just do something similar to redirect them.

What about when their behavior requires more than non-progressive interventions? When, you have tried the latter several times and in many ways, then it is a good time to move on to progressive consequences. These are part of the system that you create in your home, classroom and school. This system is a step by step procedure that is explicitly taught and explained to the children. Consistency is a key element when implementing this system.

In the classroom or school, you could explain it this way: "After I give you several reminders and prompts to follow behavior expectations, I will move on to our progressive consequence system. So, first, I will give you a rule reminder. After that, I will give you a total of three verbal warnings—for the same misbehavior. After the third verbal warning, I will contact your parents for a conference. If, after I contact your parents and confer with them, you repeat the same misbehavior, then I will have to refer you to the office. This is the process I will follow when you are not following behavior expectations. I am positive that you are all capable of following behavior expectations, and I will do all that I can to help you and to remind you to behave well; but when you continue to misbehave, this will be a choice that you have made, and we will have to follow through with our consequence system."

Whenever I had to redirect my students many times, and then followed through with the consequence system, I always made sure to keep calm and to communicate the next action steps calmly to students. They need to understand that when you follow through with the consequence process, it is not to get revenge or to punish them, but rather it is the natural procedure for certain choices that they chose to make. Look at Tool 7.4 for a visual of the School/Classroom Progressive Consequence System.

With my own children, I usually resort to non-progressive interventions to redirect them. When I tell them that I have now moved onto the progressive consequence system, and will give them the first reminder, and maybe a first warning, they take it seriously. My children know that I am very consistent and will follow the system with fidelity, step by step. This is when they realize that they do not want the consequences to progress further, and they do make a strong effort to change their behavior and behave appropriately. Look at Tool 7.3 for a visual of the Home Progressive Consequence System.

After years of implementation with my children who are now eight and thirteen, they do not require that many interventions for them to be redirected back to the right track, and I rarely need to move onto the progressive system any more.

Look at the figures in the Tool section. These are helpful visuals for the non-progressive and progressive consequence systems. When it comes to implementing the consequence system at home, there is no need to go through the 'Contact Parents' stage, since you are the parent! But, this is the stage where my husband and I (or one of us if the other is away) would hold a conference with the child. If we were to move to the last stage, which would be an 'office referral' at school, this is where we would take away something that our children like—such as their PlayStation time, iPad time, etc. This could be anything that means a lot to your children. Losing something they value for a certain period of time would be highly effective in changing their behavior. Just remember to implement the consequence calmly, objectively and consistently.

Several years ago, when I began this system with my children, they would reach a point where they would actually lose valuable time with their electronics (which mean the most to them). They would cry and beg for hours. I would remain calm and would express to them that I am sorrowful too that they have to go through this. I communicated this kindly and reminded them that I was only following the consequence system that we had all learned about and agreed on before. I communicated to them that I loved them a lot and that the consequence was a natural progression for their choices. I always found myself apologizing, too! Eventually, they accepted the situation, and actually paid their time with dignity! This strategy also developed in them a better sense of time, and they learned how to read the clock to figure out when the consequence would be over.

After years of implementing this system with fidelity, my husband and I can truly say that our children can easily pick up on initial non-progressive cues, and maybe even initial stages of the progressive consequence system, before they decide to improve their behavior and make better choices.

When I was a teacher, I implemented this system consistently with my students. With all these different strategies, I never needed to reach the point where they were referred to the office. What I realized also was that teachers who reached that point where they punished their students by sending them to the office, was that they were simply being reactive. They were fed up with the student and felt that the punishment would help relieve their own anger and frustration as teachers, because they 'kicked them out of the classroom'. So what did they achieve? They eliminated the problem temporarily, but they did not solve it.

I understand that it takes a lot of effort to implement all these strategies and to follow the system consistently. This amount of effort is discouraging for many. But, think of it this way: you became a teacher because you are a person who cares about others; you enjoy helping others gain knowledge and skills; you rejoice in the success and gains of others because it makes YOU feel accomplished and successful, too. So you are educating others to equip them for their future, to help create a better, more successful world. But is success based solely on academics? Isn't success based on character, morality and behavior? Isn't your role to educate children to become better members in the future society? Isn't this based on how they behave as civilized society members more than what creations they will make?

Children who are taught academics without behavior might end up using their knowledge for the wrong purposes. For example, if a child is taught math and business skills that will develop his ability to become a successful businessman, but fails to learn how to be an honest and honorable member of society, this person might end up creating businesses where he or she steals or sells illegitimate products. What about a child who becomes a scientist but fails to learn how to be peace-loving and compassionate? This person might invent dangerous products which could hurt or destroy others.

Making the effort now to develop universal values and positive behaviors in children, will definitely pay off in the future. This is how you would be educating children for a better world. It's all about laying the foundation for children to stay on track and to support them every step of the way until they are adults and on their own. It is not about 'fixing' all the misbehaviors as much as it is supporting them to do the right thing.

When a child struggles in reading, you help them by going back to the basics and teaching them phonics and decoding skills. You are supporting them to read well. What about when a child struggles with behavior? Support them by going back to the basics and teaching them the importance of behaving well, how to behave in the right way, what it looks like, how positively it will impact the self and others, and by providing them with tips and reminders to help them get back on track.

I met with a teacher once to provide him with feedback from an observation I had made in one of his classes. His positive interactions ratio with the students was high; he did an excellent job interacting positively with students, praising their efforts and acknowledging their on-task behavior. On the other hand, the engagement level of his students was quite low. Students were not following the classroom expectations, even though the teacher was interacting positively with them.

After I shared the results with him, he asked me, "So, what should I do? What would fix this? How can I ensure they are all engaged and following expectations?"

When teachers ask me such questions, I could easily tell them what to do and how to behave with their students, but I always choose to throw the question back at them and find out what they think they should do. So I asked him, "What do you think you should do to make sure all your students are following expectations?"

He paused and then said, "I should go back to the basics and reteach expectations."

"That is a great plan. Do you feel you made enough effort initially to teach behavior expectations to your students?"

"Not really. I should have stressed it more. I think I should have spent more time and effort to teach, reteach and remind students how to behave. I feel I should have been consistent with students who were not following classroom expectations, and not just ignored their undesirable behaviors."

Lay the foundation for students to behave well. Go back to basics when they forget or fail. Give them the tips and reminders they need. Follow the systems in the TOOLS section on the next few pages, consistently and with fidelity. Do your part. Fulfill your role and responsibility as an educator.

TOOLS

I have included the non-progressive and progressive correction system that you could use to correct any misbehavior. They are created as a helpful visual, for use at home and in the classroom.

TOOL 7.1

Non-Progressive Consequence System

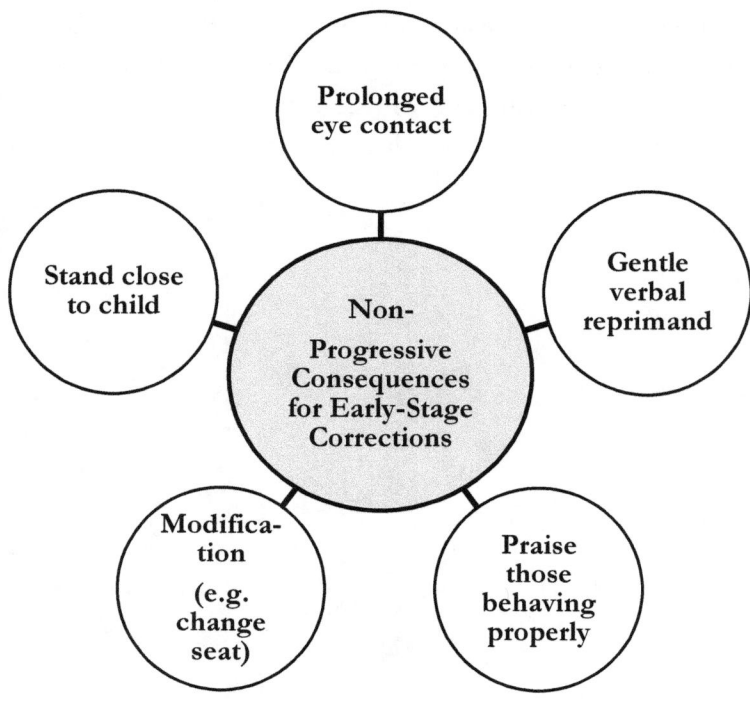

TOOL 7.2

This model serves to point out to the child that their behavior is not in sync with expectations, and reminds them of the expected behavior by verbally redirecting them to what their behavior should look like in alignment with the agreed upon values. Just like with the PLP model, the PLREP model touches the core of the child and improves their intrinsic motivation to get back on the right track. It is important to keep in mind that every time you address a child, you need to say their name first. This helps secure their attention and addresses what you are saying directly to them.

PLREP Model to Verbally Redirect Behavior

POINT OUT the undesirable behavior

LINK it to the values

REDIRECT to the desired behavior

ENCOURAGE to Motivate and Achieve Compliance

PRAISE the Desired Behavior

PLREP Model to Verbally Redirect Behavior

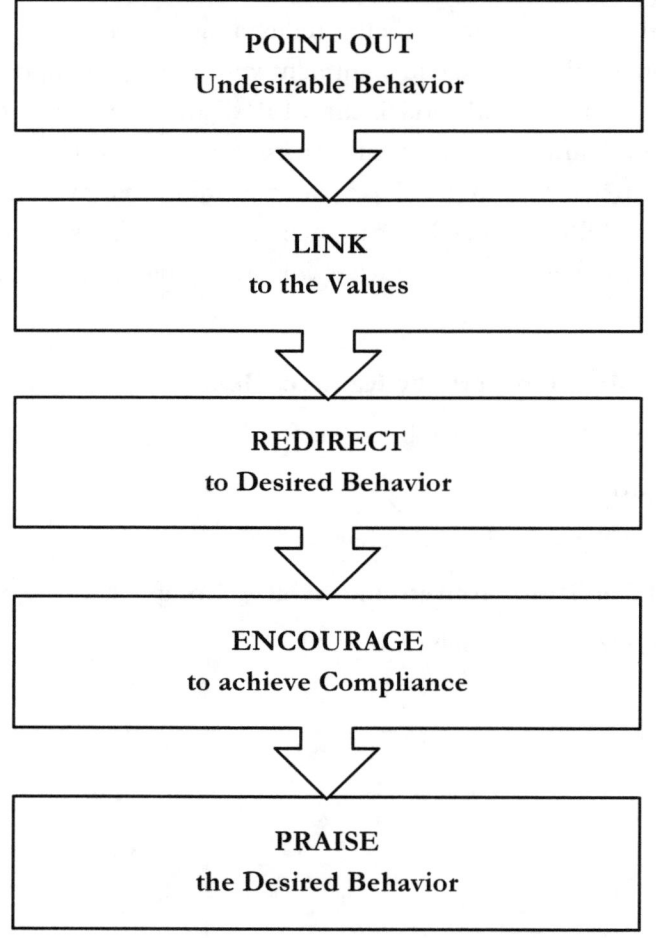

POINT OUT
Undesirable Behavior

LINK
to the Values

REDIRECT
to Desired Behavior

ENCOURAGE
to achieve Compliance

PRAISE
the Desired Behavior

Example – At Home

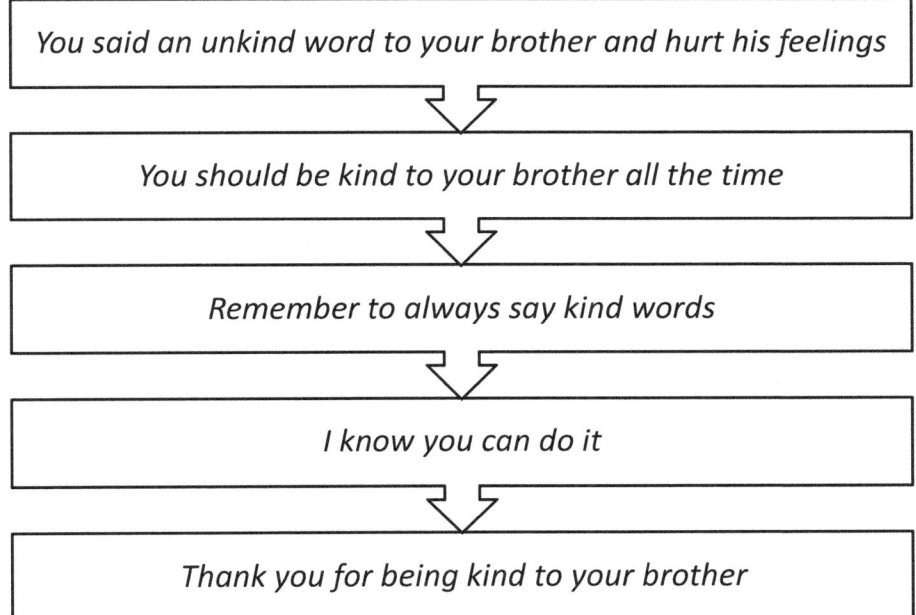

Example – At School

When I gave out the assignment, you started chatting with your partner instead of working

⬇

You are not showing responsibility

⬇

When assignments are handed out, you need to show responsibility by working immediately

⬇

I know you can behave responsibly

⬇

Thank you for working responsibly

TOOL 7.3

HOME Progressive Consequence System

Make sure you establish a Positive, Proactive & Preventive Environment where expectations are taught & reviewed regularly. Intervene with non-progressive corrections prior to following the progressive system.

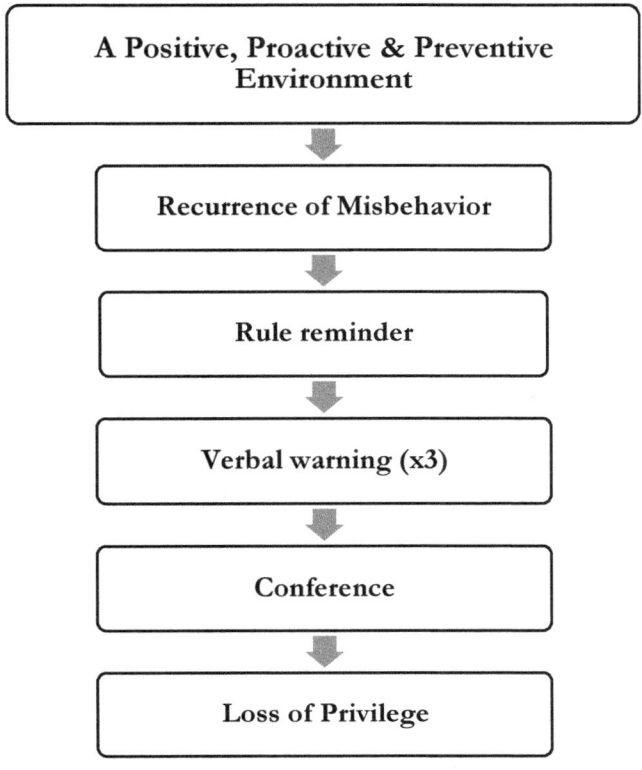

TOOL 7.4

SCHOOL / CLASSROOM Progressive Consequence System

Make sure you establish a Positive, Proactive & Preventive Environment where expectations are taught & reviewed regularly. Intervene with non-progressive corrections prior to following the progressive system.

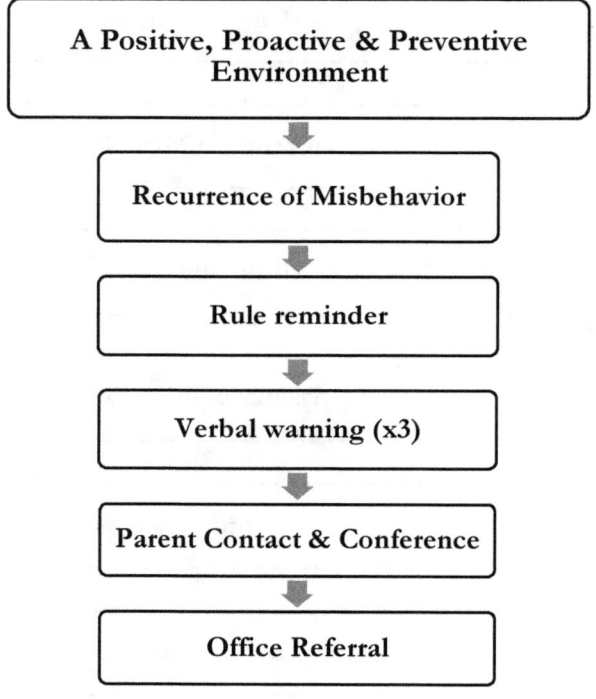

Chapter Eight
EVOLVE AND TRANSFORM

We dream of a better world...and we can make it happen.
Change must start from within us.

Change Thyself, Change Behavior, Change the World

How do you feel right now?

Do you feel more positive?

What changes did you feel you experienced?

What beliefs have remained the same?

Have all the discussions, lessons, tools and examples inspired

you to follow positive practices with your children or students?

What was mind-opening for you while reading this book?

What insights have you gained?

Do you feel hopeful?

Are you strong and ready enough to take this challenge and

make this effort, for a better home and school environment

and for a better world?

Are you able to point out what was going wrong with your

behavior management practices?

Were you able to receive affirmations that you have been doing the right thing with your children or students? What are your beliefs and attitudes about change, growth and development? Have you gained an awareness about the power you hold in influencing children? Do you feel a mental transformation? How strongly do you now believe in the power of positive behavior support?

You have read this entire book. You asked yourself reflective questions and questioned your previous views, opinions and habits. You assessed your practices as a parent and as an educator. You learned lessons about becoming better and more attentive listeners. You discovered the importance of creating strong connections. You understood what it means to interact positively, and the power of positivity in growing our minds and relationships with children. You learned about how significant it is to tap into our spring of positive emotions to become better and happier individuals and care providers for our children. You have learned all this, and much more. Your awareness has grown profoundly, and your cognitive mindset has been deeply challenged. This is the transformational reality that you have experienced.

Educators choose their career because they are humanitarians at heart, seeking to grow young minds into ones that will reign the world with positivity, compassion, leadership, justice, peace, success, hope, freedom, and much, much more.

Remember, we do not aim to create robots who exhibit appropriate behaviors for the sake of conformity. We want them to grow in their moral development and truly believe that they are responsible citizens with social responsibilities that will affect their families, communities, countries and worlds.

Let them question why they are expected to be this way and why they need to follow behavior expectations. Cultivate their "Whys" and allow them to question, be skeptical, and arrive at answers through thoughtful and respectful discussions.

Empower your children and students by listening to their thoughts and beliefs, by respecting them as individuals, by interacting positively with them, by trusting them and apologizing to them, and by believing that they will be successful.

For a little while, stop teaching how to write an expository essay, and discuss the power of being positive, the importance of being honorable, the meaning of values, the reasons why we should follow behavior expectations, the consequences of our choices, the integral significance of assessing and reflecting on our behaviors and actions, the value of growth and development, and the true meaning of success, individually and collectively.

Do not expect all your children and students to be the same. Each individual is unique. Listen to each of them and provide them with what they need. Do not penalize children who made bad choices in the past. Always open a new, blank page and encourage them to start anew. Tell them you believe in them. You are unaware of what they have been through or what growing up was like for them. They might have been privileged with material riches, but may have missed out on social connections. Be the heart that listens to them and makes them feel that they are worthy individuals.

When we make the choice to become parents or educators, WE make this choice. So we should be fully responsible for our actions towards our children and students.

You have the power to change children and change futures. When you are old and retired, give yourself the chance to look back and rejoice in the smiles you put on children's faces and the hearts that you touched with your acts of active listening, strong connections, positive interactions, teachings and motivational strategies. Think about the children you prepared for a better world, that you took part in shaping. Do not seek immediate results; seek intrinsic gratification for the remarkable changes you have made with individuals and that you continue to make, no matter how small. Begin with yourself. Change your behavior to positively impact the behavior of children.

Take pride in your achievements. Do not despair if you make mistakes; we all do and we always will. But those of us who evaluate their actions, contemplate on what they did, and strive to make better choices are those individuals that will truly appreciate the gratifying feelings of having made a difference in the world.

TOOL 8.1

COMPLETE:

Transformation Model for Positive Behavior Management

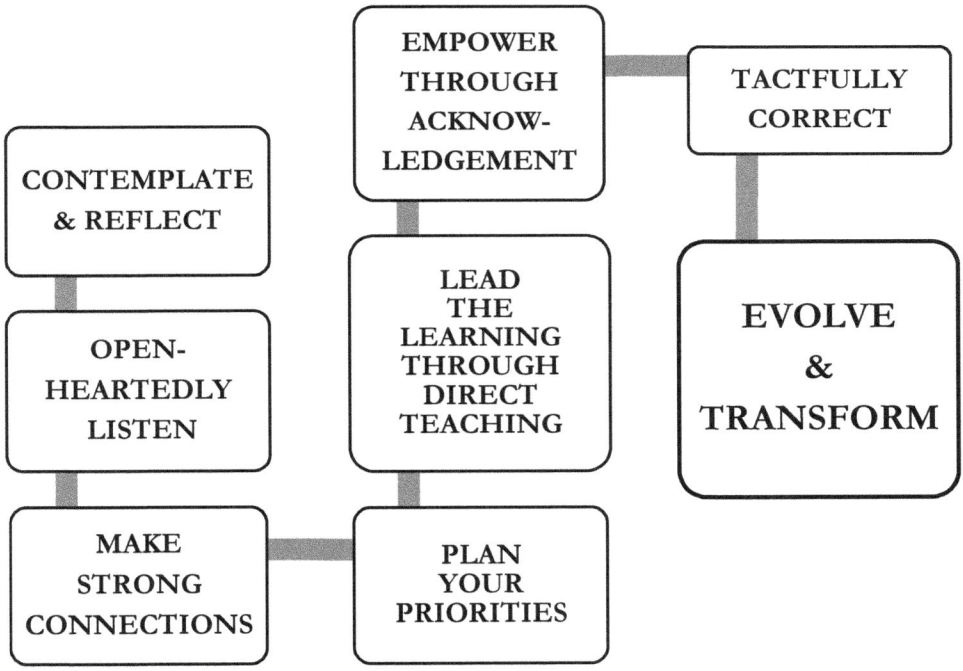

COMPLETE

TRANSFORMATION MODEL
FOR POSITIVE BEHAVIOR MANAGEMENT
Summary of Implementation

Use the model and table to help you capture the main steps to guide you in your implementation. As a summary, I wrote a sentence for each step. I would like you to add your own action steps for each. This tool would serve as your guide and daily reminder. Use affirmative statements beginning with 'I will…' and make sure they are phrased positively.

Begin by writing a general statement describing your vision for yourself, your home, classroom, or school. Include the values you have chosen. You may fill in the blanks below to create your vision statement. Make sure it is phrased positively. This statement will show your goal and purpose and will help you create the commitment necessary to be successful in implementing the action steps and achieving your goals to live according to your vision.

I value _____, _____, _____, _____,
and _____.
In my _____ (home/classroom/school), we value
_____, _____, _____, _____,
and _____ (write the values you listed in the first
statement).
These values will bring _____
and make us feel _____.
I am committed to these values because I am
accountable for myself, my children and/or my students.
I will support my children and/or my students
to live by these values and to be their best so that
they could be successful. I want to help create
a better world.

1. **Contemplate and Reflect:** Reflect upon your own past experiences and examine your current beliefs.

   _____

   _____

   _____

2. **Openheartedly Listen:** Get in-tune with your inner self by looking within yourself, assessing and reflecting on your actions, attitudes and feelings.

   _____

   _____

   _____

3. **Make Strong Connections:** Build strong relationships with children based on respect, honesty, openness and support.

   _____

   _____

   _____

4. **Plan Your Priorities:** Plan what behaviors you would like to see in your children, based on the values you would like to instill.

   _____

   _____

   _____

5. **Lead the Learning through DIRECT Teaching:** Teach the specific desired behaviors directly and explicitly.

_____

_____

_____

6. **Empower Through Acknowledgement:** Catch your children being good and let them know what they did right by interacting positively with them. Follow the PLP Model to verbally acknowledge behavior.

_____

_____

_____

7. **Tactfully Correct:** Intervene immediately for early-stage corrections and follow the PLREP Model to verbally redirect behavior.

_____

_____

_____

8. **Evolve and Transform:** Follow the COMPLETE Transformation Model for behavior management.

_____

_____

_____

"*The COMPLETE Model* is exactly that, a supreme and exciting package to assist, nurture and enable positive child development. What makes this resource stand out is that the author not only provides user-friendly strategies but encourages the reader to also evolve, transform, look within, to focus on the positives, to utilise a different lens where we can only see good behaviour. Thank you Dina for creating this solid publication that can be utilised at home and school by any pro-active carer/educator, the tools benefiting not only students but the adults involved in their behaviour management journey."
— *Josie Santomauro, International Author, Presenter & Consultant on Autism Spectrum Disorders. Australia.*

"This book is jam-packed with ideas, examples, and tips that can immediately be taken directly to the classroom or home. Ms. Al-Hidiq Zebib has provided not only educators and parents with a how-to manual for raising and teaching children through positive behavior management, but her ideas and techniques are useful to all people. As a former educator, this book would have been extremely helpful to me in classroom management. I think back on my time in the classroom, and wish I had this book available to me as a resource…I highly recommend "The COMPLETE Model for Positive Behavior Management" by Dina Al-Hidiq Zebib for not only teachers and parents, but for all people in general, as well. This book is truly a gem!"
— *Christine Watson, Reader Views. USA*

"The author is a longtime coach, educator, and mother who is well-suited to ask the difficult questions that drive inner reflection and positive change…the author successfully provides a practical and actionable step-by-step guide to implementing her suggested strategies. Dina Al-Hidiq Zebib provides pathways for active engagement with the material, which challenges the reader to embrace personal growth and implement positive change…a highly recommended, worthwhile read for both parents and educators."
— *Jacquelyn Gilchrist, The US Review of Books*

For more information
about the author and her work, visit:
www.dinaalhidiq.com

For coaching, training and consultation
requests, email:
dina@dinaalhidiq.com

www.ingramcontent.com/pod-product-compliance
Lightning Source LLC
Chambersburg PA
CBHW061658120626
46550CB00003B/992